Isaiah 53 Explained

By Dr. Mitch Glaser

ISAIAH 53 EXPLAINED

Library of Congress Cataloging in Publication Data
Main entry under title:
Isaiah 53 Explained
ISBN 1-882675-11-8

Cover design by Maralynn Rochat

TABLE OF CONTENTS

Foreword

One chapter really can change your life!

That chapter is Isaiah 53, and the best-selling book in which it is found is the Bible—the Hebrew Scriptures, often described as the Old Testament.

This brief volume is written primarily for those who are not religious. Since Isaiah 53 is found in the Hebrew Scriptures, much of what you are about to read is written with the Jewish reader in mind. However, this is not intended to be exclusively so. Like Jerusalem—a Jewish city important to many faiths—the Hebrew Scriptures, originally Jewish documents, are considered to be holy writings by Christians as well. The Old Testament is also referenced in the Koran. Therefore, even though this book is primarily written for Jewish people, hopefully it will be read and understood by those of a variety of faiths: Christian, Muslim, Buddhist, Hindu and those who do not claim allegiance to any formal religion, but are looking to deepen their relationship with God.

There are a number of reasons why Isaiah 53 can change your life. As a chapter in the Jewish Bible, Isaiah 53 is part of the book that describes our history, ethics, religion and the very basis for our Jewish heritage. There is also considerable information in the Hebrew Scriptures regarding God's love and plan for the Gentile nations. Whether or not you are Jewish, whether or not you are religious, I hope you will discover that reading and understanding Isaiah chapter 53 will change your life.

Allow me to offer a few compelling reasons why I hope you will find Isaiah 53 meaningful:

- This chapter will help you understand some things about yourself—especially regarding your relationship to the God of Abraham, Isaac and Jacob.

- This chapter will demonstrate that the Bible can be trusted.

- This chapter will introduce you to God, who predicts the future and also brings it to pass.

- This chapter will help shape your expectation of who the Messiah would be. You will discover how this chapter has been fulfilled in the life of the One whom many call "the greatest Jew who ever lived."

This book was written by a Messianic Jew—a Jewish person who believes that Jesus (Yeshua) is the Messiah of Israel and the fulfillment of Isaiah 53—and one whose life was completely changed as a result.

Having been raised in a traditional Jewish home, I fully understand the challenges of keeping an open mind to the possibility that Jesus is the Messiah. So many of my fellow Jews are searching for a deeper spirituality and desire an intimate personal relationship with God. Many of us have not found this within the Jewish religion, but we would never consider detaching ourselves from the Jewish community.

When I came to believe that Yeshua was the Messiah many years ago, I certainly had no intention of abandoning my Jewishness. I was looking for an authentic spirituality, and I imagine you might be interested in the same thing. I hope you might be willing to put aside—at least for a moment—the common belief that you cannot be Jewish and believe in Jesus.

After all, if one of our greatest Jewish prophets predicted the Messianic details that Yeshua ultimately fulfills, then we would certainly have the basis to believe that one can be Jewish and believe in Yeshua.

More than anything, I hope that as you read this brief volume, your soul will be deeply touched by God. I pray that your spiritual search for a deeper and more intimate relationship with the Creator will become a reality in your life as it has in mine. There is no relationship in the world more fulfilling—or one that brings greater joy and satisfaction—than connection with the God of Abraham, Isaac and Jacob.

The purpose of this book is not to persuade you to change religions, but rather to discover a new relationship with the One who made you in His image and created you for this relationship. Not knowing God is like not knowing your mother or father; it leaves a hole in your soul that can only be filled by discovering where you have come from. Without knowing God, it is difficult to answer the fundamental questions of life: Why am I here? What is my purpose for living? How should I live my life in a way that gives me the most fulfillment and helps me to be a better person? These are the questions that either plague us or propel us into the arms of our Creator.

May the Lord enlighten your path and give you the insight to understand Isaiah chapter 53—and to find a new and personal relationship with the God who made you and loves you.

Dr. Mitch Glaser

Jerusalem
May 2010

INTRODUCTION

If you are Jewish, whether or not you are observant, you probably have a sense of identification with the history of our people. You are likely reluctant to do anything that you believe would cause you to step away from or dishonor that heritage. This is what crossed my mind when someone suggested to me that Jesus was the promised Messiah of Israel. I thought: "You will never get me to believe that unless you demonstrate it to me from within the Jewish world. Show it to me from our own sacred writings, and then I'll look at it more closely. Don't quote the New Testament to me!"

My unspoken challenge was answered. One of the pivotal passages of the Hebrew Bible that revolutionized my thinking on the subject was the 53rd chapter of the Book of Isaiah. Believe me, it was not easy to believe that Jesus was the Messiah and the fulfillment of all we hoped for as Jews throughout the centuries! It was a struggle—especially because this ancient prophecy describes the Messiah in a way that I did not expect. Instead of the Messiah coming as a warrior king conquering our enemies (as I was raised to believe), this chapter portrays Him as a humble man who ultimately suffered for the sins of all humanity at the cost of His own life.

At first, it just did not add up. Maybe you feel the same way. Jesus—or as we call Him by His Hebrew name, Yeshua—might seem to be the most unlikely of all persons to fit your image of the Messiah. And I had another problem—it was also hard for me to consider

11

Jesus objectively because of the harm that has been done to the Jewish people in His name by His so-called followers. It is natural to be suspicious of someone whose supposed devotees have behaved so destructively.

On top of that was the undeniable fact that the Jesus I grew up avoiding seemed, quite frankly, to be the furthest thing from a Jewish Messiah that I could possibly imagine. Let's face it—most of the images that are portrayed of Yeshua are alien to Jewish life and culture. That's why Isaiah 53 was such an eye-opener.

Many Jewish people, even those who are religious, are unfamiliar with Isaiah chapter 53 because Isaiah 53 is not included in the weekly *Haftarah*[1] portions read in the synagogue.

I would not suggest that omitting this chapter from the weekly *Haftarah* portion was an intentional act of conspiracy, yet it is somewhat mysterious as to why the cyclical synagogue readings go from Isaiah chapter 52 to chapter 54. We are all free to make up our own minds about the reason why our sages chose to skip over the 53rd chapter.

It's true that sincere Jewish scholars have wrestled with Isaiah 53 and have chosen not to interpret this passage as fulfilled by Jesus of Nazareth. Perhaps some have chosen not to pursue this possibility because of the potentially severe social penalties they might suffer.

I ask you to try for the moment to put aside any prejudices—however justifiable—and carefully consider what follows. I am hoping that you will have an open mind and that you will draw your own conclusions as you read it. Please pray that God would reveal to you the truth about this intriguing text.

ISAIAH 53

1 *"Who would have believed our report?*
   And to whom has the arm of the LORD been revealed?

2 *For he shot up right forth as a sapling,*
   and as a root out of a dry ground;
   he had no form nor comeliness,
   that we should look upon him,
   nor beauty that we should delight in him.

3 *He was despised, and forsaken of men,*
   a man of pains, and acquainted with disease,
   and as one from whom men hide their face:
   he was despised, and we esteemed him not.

4 *Surely our diseases he did bear,*
   and our pains he carried;
   whereas we did esteem him stricken,
   smitten of God, and afflicted.

5 *But he was wounded because of our transgressions,*
   he was crushed because of our iniquities:
   the chastisement of our welfare was upon him,
   and with his stripes we were healed.

6 *All we like sheep did go astray,*
   we turned every one to his own way;
   and the LORD has made to light on him the iniquity of us all.

7 *He was oppressed, though he humbled himself*
   and opened not his mouth;
   as a lamb that is led to the slaughter,
   and as a sheep that before her shearers is dumb;
   yea, he opened not his mouth.

8   By oppression and judgment he was taken away,
    and with his generation who did reason?
    for he was cut off out of the land of the living,
    for the transgression of my people to whom the stroke was due.

9   And they made his grave with the wicked,
    and with the rich his tomb;
    although he had done no violence,
    neither was any deceit in his mouth."

10 Yet it pleased the LORD to crush him by disease;
    to see if his soul would offer itself in restitution,
    that he might see his seed, prolong his days,
    and that the purpose of the LORD
    might prosper by his hand:

11 Of the travail of his soul he shall see to the full,
    even My servant, who by his knowledge
    did justify the Righteous One to the many,
    and their iniquities he did bear.

12 Therefore will I divide him a portion among the great,
    and he shall divide the spoil with the mighty;
    because he bared his soul unto death,
    and was numbered with the transgressors;
    yet he bore the sin of many,
    and made intercession for the transgressors.

In this book, we will examine the historical trustworthiness
of the Old and New Testaments, learn about the nature of
prophecy and the concept of atonement and compare the
life and character of Yeshua with the specific details found in
Isaiah chapter 53. Come on this journey with me—all you
need is an open mind and an open heart!

CHAPTER 1:
I'M JEWISH...NOW WHAT?

If most Jewish people today were to be completely honest, we might admit to being embarrassed by the idea that we are God's chosen people. It makes us uncomfortable to think there is something innately special about being Jewish.

Certainly religious Jews have an easier time accepting that the Jewish people are God's chosen people. According to the more religious Jewish community, we are chosen to be faithful to the God of Israel as we live in obedience to His Laws revealed in the Torah given at Mount Sinai.

Yet most of us are not "religious." In fact, we may be disturbed by the apparent "elitism" of our fellow Jews who embrace this belief that the Jewish people are God's chosen people.

To think that we as a people are especially chosen by God seems narrow-minded and arrogant when viewed through the lens of our modern multicultural world. We can easily accept our uniqueness as an ethnic group. We can celebrate the beauty of our heritage, just like Polish Americans, Italian Americans, African Americans and Latin Americans, but to view ourselves as "chosen" seems to take uniqueness to an unwarranted degree.

The Burden of Being Chosen

What makes the Jewish people unique among the peoples of the world? I know this is not a question we ask ourselves or others every day, but it is something most of us who were raised as Jews still want to understand better. We might not let others know how important this is to us, but we know we are Jewish and, in some ways, it has cost us a lot—though it cost those who came before us much more. We know about the *pogroms* and the Crusades from the more distant past. And even in the 21st century, we Jews live with an ever-present awareness of the Holocaust. We ourselves might not be Holocaust survivors or the children of survivors, but we knew of survivors and have seen pictures of those who did not survive. In many ways, the Holocaust has shaped our lives and identities.

The survival of the Jewish people is important to us because we are Jewish. Most of us want to see our people survive, and our history and culture thrive. We have lost so much in the past century that the survival of our people, nation, culture and religion—even if we are not especially religious—is important to us as Jews. Wouldn't you agree?

What does it mean to be Jewish, aside from the variety of inside jokes that naturally pass through our minds when we consider this question? Chicken soup for a cold, getting straight As in school—we all know the shtick! But I believe we also want answers that go deeper and are more thoughtful.

For the most part, our Jewishness still determines how we handle the various rites of passage from childhood to adulthood. Being Jewish implies a certain way of relating to the world. Although we hold to the cultural norms that our mothers taught us, we suspect that there is much more to what it means to be a Jew.

Maybe one of the most important questions to ask is, What does it mean to be "chosen?"

One of the clearest statements of Jewish ambivalence towards "chosenness" is found in a poignant moment in *Fiddler on the Roof:* Tevye the milkman lifts his eyes to heaven and says, "I know, I know. We are Your chosen people. But, once in a while, can't You choose somebody else?"

The Jewish understanding of being chosen by God has been elusive and mysterious. Being chosen seems to have increased our burden far more than our joy. It has brought more trouble than triumph and has been a root cause for ongoing persecution. Some Gentiles have used Jewish "chosenness" as a basis for antisemitism.

This has especially reflected poorly on relationships between Jews and "Christians," even more so than between Jews and Muslims. An unfortunate sense of competition has developed over the centuries between these two great world religions that both understand themselves to be people chosen by God.

This tension has led to a misunderstanding within historical Christianity that the Jewish people are no longer chosen and are, in fact, judged as a nation for rejecting Jesus. It is this belief that has caused many "Christians" throughout the centuries to view mistreatment of Jews as service to God. This might not be as widespread today, but the residual tension continues and affects our mutual understanding.

Is it any wonder that we have a hard time entertaining the thought that our own Bible would predict the very same Messiah who is viewed as the founder of Christianity?[2] Given our history, it is almost impossible for us to understand "Christianity" as a Jewish movement that is also welcoming of Gentiles. If we believe that Jesus is the Jewish Messiah, then we would have to rework our understanding of Christianity and view it as something Jewish rather than as something foreign and Gentile. This would be very difficult for most of us.

Historically, we have had a difficult time even considering the idea that the Messiah was to suffer and die before He would reign as king. As you will see in chapter 10, there are strains of this thinking in the *Mishnah* and other rabbinic writings that actually suggest this very same thing. But I know that it is hard to open our minds to this possibility if it might lead us to accept the very Messiah embraced by those who persecuted our forefathers.

This makes it very difficult for us to take an objective look at Isaiah chapter 53. Furthermore, if Jesus is the Jewish Messiah and is also the Messiah for the Gentiles, then what exactly is unique about our being chosen by God? What then is the destiny and purpose of the Jewish people?

CHOSEN WITHOUT A CHOOSER

There is a Maccabi Beer advertisement popular in Israel in which the tag line reads, "Maccabi Beer—the beer that Chosen People choose." The very *raison d'etre* for the Jewish people is reduced to a pithy marketing statement used to sell beer! However, this shouldn't be surprising. The tag line was surely penned by a Jewish writer who was uncertain of what it actually means to be the chosen people.

Today, the very notion of one people claiming to be chosen is repugnant. All of the great political movements of the recent past, from the French Revolution onward, were designed to break down the notion of a privileged class—and the idea of a "chosen" people is considered regressive.

There were Jewish people at the forefront of these social movements, from France to Russia to the United States. In fact, the "classless society" is often a far more cherished ideal for Jewish people than the thought of being chosen by God for a special purpose.

As Jewish Americans, we are proud to say that one of our fundamental ideals is to treat all people as equals. Why then should one group be viewed as chosen? It goes against the very philosophical fabric of our society and that of most Western countries.

The question of "chosenness" is also a cause for deep self-questioning by Jewish people. What impact would it have if we really believed that there is a God who created us as individuals and as a people with a divine purpose? We would certainly want to discover what that divine purpose is for our lives, would we not?

WHERE DO WE TURN FOR ANSWERS?

The very idea that we have been chosen implies that there is a Chooser. How can we try to understand our chosenness without coming to terms with the Chooser?

We know that the Jewish people are unique. We have a distinct history and certain common cultural traits that are intertwined with those of the nations where our people have settled over the centuries. Whether we are Sephardi or Ashkenazi, whether we are from the former Soviet Union, Israel, Poland or North Africa, we are bound to one another as Jews. However, the notion of "chosenness" is more than religious celebrations, foods and the bonds of a common national history.

There is something far deeper that underlies our heritage: it is the idea that we have been chosen by the Creator for a holy and special purpose. And until we discover this purpose, by first of all building a relationship with the One who chose us, we will not be fulfilled as Jews or as human beings.

Perhaps you have already tried to determine the significance of being a Jew without reading the Bible, and have found the answers to be fleeting and shallow. This is because it is only through understanding the Bible can we understand the mystery of our "chosenness," as this is where the idea is first mentioned and developed. In reading the Scriptures, we discover the God who chose us and the reasons why He did, as well as His purposes for the nations of the world.

This will be a search well worth pursuing, and doing so will enrich your life. When we understand and embrace the "chosenness" of the Jewish people as described in the Bible, we will begin to comprehend what it means to be Jewish. However, this search might lead to a surprising destination—so let's keep an open mind!

In fact, it is only by understanding our being chosen by God that we can begin to fathom the miracle of our ongoing national existence. There's no doubt in my mind that in the reasonable course of history, the Jewish people should have been obliterated. Yet not only have we survived, but we have also thrived; today we find ourselves back in our land, speaking our language and having a profound influence on the world stage.

Mark Twain, an agnostic and skeptic, knew that the continued existence of the Jewish people was unusual and remarkable. He wrote in 1899:

> The Egyptian, the Babylonian and the Persian rose, filled the planet with sound and splendor, then faded to dream stuff and passed away; the Greek and the Roman followed, and made a vast noise, and they are gone; other peoples have sprung up and held their torch high for a time, but it burned out, and they sit in twilight now, or have vanished. The Jew saw them all, beat them all, and is now what he always was, exhibiting no decadence, no infirmities of age, no weakening of his parts, no slowing of his energies, no dulling of his alert and aggressive mind. All things are mortal but the Jew; all other forces pass but he remains. What is the secret of his immortality?[3]

He wrote this half a century before the modern State of Israel was established. And even more profoundly, he wrote this prior to the Holocaust. I can only imagine what Twain would have said in light of these two events; they would have further strengthened his observation about the "immortality" of the Jewish people.

Neither the dominance of foreign nations, nor the Crusades, nor persistent persecution in Eastern Europe, nor ultimately Hitler's final and destructive solution to the "Jewish question" could destroy the Jewish people as a whole.

Even if we have not shown up in a synagogue since the day we heard our rabbis say, "Today you are a man (or a woman)," we cannot deny that there is something supernatural about the ongoing existence of the Jewish people.

How is it possible to explain this modern miracle outside of the fact that there is a God who chose our people and continues to preserve our nation? The continued existence of the Jewish people and the establishment of the modern State of Israel argue persuasively and passionately for the existence of the God of Abraham, Isaac and Jacob. And since the future of Israel was established and assured by the Scriptures—these ancient documents compiled into what we now call the *Tanakh* (the Jewish Bible or the Old Testament) must be taken very seriously.

THE BIBLICAL PERSPECTIVE

In order to understand the idea of "chosenness" in Judaism, we need to examine the biblical passages where it is described. Though we might attend synagogue here and there and have a great appreciation for our history and religion, we still might be unfamiliar with the actual biblical foundations upon which the idea of our being chosen rests.

Some of us who are fairly typical post-bar-mitzvah dropouts recognize in the depths of our souls that without understanding the Jewish Bible, it would be very difficult to fully understand who we are as Jews. We simply cannot adequately answer the question of our "chosenness" without taking into consideration the existence of a God who is capable of choosing and the book in which the spiritual origins for our peoplehood have been described. Where else can we turn for answers?

Perhaps you believe that the Bible is just a book of Jewish history. Maybe you see it as the basic and fundamental religious document of the Jewish people—as well as of Christians and Muslims, for that matter. Perhaps to you it is simply a collection of interesting readings: ethical and moral aphorisms, beautiful Psalms and poetry and the wisdom and knowledge of our people accumulated over the centuries.

In the chapters that follow, we will examine the evidence for the reliability and credibility of the Scriptures. But no matter how you currently view the Bible, I am sure that as you read, your soul will be enriched and your Jewish identity will deepen. At the very least, you will better understand the source of this concept of Jewish "chosenness."

THE CHOOSING OF ABRAHAM

The choosing of the Jewish people began with the choosing of a man and a woman: Abraham (Abram at the time) and Sarah (then Sarai). These Semitic nomads were called by God to be the parents of a new nation. According to the text, their chances of becoming parents to anyone—let alone a nation—were unlikely. It is interesting that God did far more than simply choose the Jewish people; He actually *created* a nation from a man and a woman who were far beyond the years of natural childbearing. This first encounter between God and Abram is recorded in Genesis 12:1-3:

> Now the LORD said unto Abram: "Get thee out of thy country, and from thy kindred, and from thy father's house, unto the land that I will show thee. And I will make of thee a great nation, and I will bless thee, and make thy name great; and be thou a blessing. And I will bless them that bless you, and him that curses you will I curse; and in you shall all the families of the earth be blessed."

God promised to create a country in which this miraculously created people would live, and He even set the borders for the new country. Note the boundaries outlined in Genesis 15:18:

> In that day the LORD made a covenant with Abram, saying: "Unto thy seed have I given this land, from the river of Egypt unto the great river, the river Euphrates…"

In the Book of Genesis, God asserted Himself as both Creator and Chooser of the chosen people. He promised miraculously to provide a son for Abram and Sarah and then to create a nation from their descendants. He made a number of profound personal promises to Abram as well.

However, the real focal point of the text is found in chapter 12, verse 3, where from the Creator Himself we learn of the divine rationale for the existence of the Jewish people. This fact—further confirmed in the writings of the prophets—is that the nation of Israel was created by God for the benefit of the nations of the world (goyim). The Jewish people were created by God to be a source of blessing to non-Jews!

In the books of the prophets, Israel is called to be a light to the nations and a witness to God's truth in His cosmic courtroom. Traditionally, Jewish people have understood this as God's call upon our people to bring the message of ethical monotheism to a world that worshiped a plethora of gods.

The Jewish people were called to tell the world about a good God who demanded that citizens of His righteous kingdom care for the poor and marginalized. He condemned the sacrifice of children, the institution of temple prostitution and other horrific practices performed in the name of religion that especially oppressed women, children and those deemed defenseless by the ancient world.

Even if you are an agnostic or an atheist and subscribe to more contemporary interpretations, you might still understand Israel's national mandate expressed by the author of Genesis in terms of specific obligations to bring the message of Torah ethics to a world in desperate need of *Tikkun Olam*.[4]

However, although the Jewish people were created and called by God to bring blessings to the world, we were not told specifically what these blessings might be. Shall we understand the blessings Jewish people are to bring to the world as Torah-based ethical monotheism, or is there something more?

Rabbi Saul—better known as the Apostle Paul—wrote in his letter to the early followers of Yeshua living in the region of Galatia (in Turkey) that the ultimate blessing the Jewish people would bring to the world was Yeshua the Messiah. Yeshua was a descendant of Abraham and David, a Jewish man born of a Jewish mother depicted as the Jewish Messiah for all people.

It is interesting that today more Gentiles accept the *Tanakh*, embrace ethical monotheism and believe in the principles of the Torah than anyone would have ever imagined. This could not have been accomplished if Yeshua had not been widely accepted by the Gentiles. Perhaps Rabbi Saul was not far off in describing Him as the ultimate blessing the Jewish people would give to the world.

So what's so special about being Jewish? Although our people's survival is miraculous, we were created to do much more than simply survive. God chose the Jewish people to have a relationship with Him personally and as a nation so that we would pass along the blessings of that relationship to the nations of the world. We will be happiest when we embrace that call on our people and on our lives.

Ultimately, the greatest blessing we would bring to the world would be the Messiah—but how and when would this Messiah come and bring about an age of peace and prosperity? Has it taken so long and is the world so hopeless that we should simply forget it and move on?

The Jewish people have a divine destiny and were chosen by God to bring the Messiah to the world. All else that we do may be viewed as preparing to fulfill our national destiny as God's instruments of ultimate *shalom* for the world. As Jewish people, we are at our best when we understand God's desire for our people and participate with Him in His plan.

God, in fact, planned a Messianic "surprise appearance," as the Messiah entered the scene in a wholly unforeseen way...or was it? Read on and you will see.

Chapter 2:
The Hebrew Scriptures—
More than a History Book

Have you ever read the Bible? I am sure that you had to read this national Jewish treasure if you were bar or bat mitzvahed. You probably learned biblical Hebrew and were able to recite your *Haftarah* portion to the delight of your relatives. However, you may never have read through the Bible with the intent of understanding God's purposes for humankind, for the Jewish people and for your own life.

Most of us went to Hebrew school and participated in Jewish community life because it was expected. Certainly, we may identify strongly as Jews—whether religiously or not—without regularly reading the Bible. But it cannot hurt to try to understand this timeless work, which has been at the heart of Jewish life since Mount Sinai.

Maybe it is time for you to read it as an adult, to try to comprehend the full story, and draw your own conclusions as to whether or not this book is relevant to life in the 21st century. I suspect you will be surprised!

In recent decades, many Jewish people have searched for truth outside traditional Judaism, looking to Hinduism, Buddhism and other forms of non-Jewish spirituality. This shows that we are seeking answers and searching for the deeper meaning of life. Yet all too often we have not tried to tap into our own spiritual history. Have you ever wondered why we are so reluctant to search the Hebrew Scriptures and develop a spirituality that is more in line with the history of our people?

Truth be told, most of us see the Bible as somewhat irrelevant, not something we would put in the front of our bookshelves to make sure that we have easy access to it for everyday reading.

If you have read the Bible in Hebrew in the past, you probably did not understand much of what you read. Sometimes we are raised to believe that Hebrew was a special language and that one can find meaning and receive blessings simply by repeating words that we do not understand—but that mentality has likely done more to turn us off from the Scriptures and from Judaism than to encourage us!

Before Hebrew was a modern language, it was known as a holy language—the language of prayer and religious observances, as well as of the Bible. Perhaps one of the reasons we have not searched our Bible to find a more Jewish spirituality and relationship with God is that we were simply unfamiliar with Hebrew, and never really considered sitting down and opening an English translation of the Bible.

Hebrew has made a comeback; the modern State of Israel has catapulted the Hebrew language into everyday use by a whole nation of people. Yet even if many of us learned conversational Hebrew, we still do not know an adequate amount of Hebrew to read the Bible.

These factors have all conspired to make the Bible seemingly inaccessible to the modern Jewish person.

Perhaps you view the Bible as a collection of antiquated laws that limit an individual's freedom. Religious authority can be frightening, as there are many abuses therein. People have done—and continue to do—some terrible things in the name of their god or prophet, believing that they are above the laws of common goodness and even the laws of their respective nations. Although Bible believers have also made many positive and admirable contributions to society, the bad and often the evil done while claiming the authority of the "Good Book" is sometimes overwhelming. It is unfortunate that some people use the Bible's good moral and ethical teaching as a weapon to harm others—especially those who disagree.

Yet there is a certain beauty, wholesomeness and purity that flow from the Bible. The ethical and moral lessons in the Bible teach us to be charitable, to be good husbands and wives, mothers and fathers, siblings and members of the community. It is this very biblical ethic that drives many of the marvelous philanthropic efforts of our country. If Bernie Madoff had read the Bible and taken it to heart, he would not have embarrassed his community by his cruel and heartless greed, which bankrupted so many individuals and so many Jewish social and philanthropic institutions.

There is a debate as to whether the Scriptures should be viewed as inspired by God or as written by inspired people. The expression "inspired by God" means "God-breathed." There are many excellent books written that answer this question. You will need to read the Bible and decide for yourself, but clearly, if you do believe in God and believe that He reveals Himself to mankind, then it is reasonable to think that this book, which has stood the test of time, goes beyond the best of human wisdom.

Can we explain how God could actually inspire flawed human beings to write an accurate record of His dealings with mankind? Is it possible to know for sure that when we read the verses of Scripture, we are hearing the voice of God? Even if you are unclear at this moment how you might answer these questions, you can still read the Bible with an open mind and ask God to speak to you through this book—nothing is lost by trying!

You might ask, "How can we know that the Bible we have today is the same as the one written by Moses and the prophets?" Time and space do not permit the opportunity to discuss that question in detail—but consider the exquisite attention to detail paid to the preservation and transmission of the Scriptures from generation to generation, especially before the invention of the printing press. For example, the oldest text of Isaiah 53 we have is from approximately 200 BCE; it was found in Qumran and is part of the collection of Dead Sea Scrolls. Before this discovery, the oldest text we had was from 900 CE. The two texts are virtually identical word for word, which gives powerful testimony to the care and precision of the Jewish copyists—and to the hand of God upon the process.

The key to having our lives enriched by the Scriptures is not knowing the details of how the Bible was written or transmitted, but rather allowing the meaning of its story to be our focus.

The Story Line of the Bible

It is possible that you have gone to synagogue all your life and fully understand the story line of the Bible. But if you are anything like most of us, you have not been to synagogue all that regularly and probably have never really pondered the overall story of the Bible. You might not know the basic organization of the Bible or the story line and plot of the book.

According to Jewish tradition, there are three major sections of the Bible. The first is the Torah—the five books of Moses. The second is the Prophets. The third is the Writings, which would include the Psalms and the historical books (First and Second Samuel, First and Second Kings, etc.) as well as some of the other books. There are also some smaller sections of the Bible such as the Book of Esther, with which we might be familiar because of holidays like Purim.

Though originally written on scrolls, today the Bible is not read from scrolls outside the synagogue. After the invention of the printing press, some practical individuals decided that it would be best to divide the books into chapters and verses like other types of literature for ease of use. These chapter/verse divisions sometimes seem arbitrary, but they do make for easy reference.

The first five books of the Bible tell the story from creation until Joshua, the successor to Moses. The five books of Moses, the Torah, contain the stories of Abraham, Isaac, Jacob, Joseph and their wives and children—and make any soap opera look boring! These books include the first Passover, the crossing of the Red Sea, the first Messianic promises, the binding of Isaac and so much more. Also included in the five books of Moses is the giving of the Law from Mount Sinai. Although the Temple was not yet built (there was only a traveling Tabernacle), the system of sacrifices was instituted in the five books of Moses and played a very important part in the religious life of the Jewish people.

There were also some great ideas and themes presented for the first time in the five books of Moses, including hints about the character of God—His love, holiness, power and glory. The creation of Adam and Eve and their disobedience to God's command, resulting in their banishment from the ideal place God created for them, became the basis for one of the most important parts of the Bible's story line. You see, although the first man and woman had everything, they were tempted by the "serpent" (the devil) and rebelled against God. This is one of the great running themes in the Bible: God blessing humankind and then, unfortunately, us tending to turn our backs on Him.

In fact, the whole rest of the Bible's story focuses on God's efforts to rescue (redeem) humankind, so that His creation would fulfill the destiny He desired for us. The Passover story becomes the paradigm for the story of redemption: an all-powerful God promised to save the Jewish people, deliver them from the bondage of slavery and set them free to live in the land He had promised to them. This becomes a motif for "salvation," which is a commonly-used but little-understood term. Fundamentally, salvation means to be set free from bondage to live in the spiritual freedom of God's promises and presence.

The Bible also tells the story of the creation of the Jewish people. The author described the calling of Abram, the promise of the nation and the land, the forming of a national identity in Egypt and the assurance that although the nation would go through difficulty, the mighty hand of God would uphold His people. Nothing in heaven or on earth could keep God from fulfilling His promise.

The historical books, beginning with Joshua, tell the story of the conquering of the land of Israel and the building of a nation. They speak about the establishment of a Davidic dynasty that would endure forever. This is one of the reasons why Jewish people traditionally believe that the Messiah will be a descendant of King David—and even that He would be born in David's ancestral town of Bethlehem.

The historical books tell how the Jewish people went from a tribal community, to a nation, to a subjugated people, to a people who returned to their homeland. Of course, not all of the Jewish people returned to the land of Israel after the Babylonian captivity. In 722 BCE the powerful Assyrian nation, whose capital was Nineveh (remember the story of Jonah?), attacked the northern tribes of Israel (following the reign of David's son Solomon, there had been a split in the nation) and ten of the tribes were allegedly "lost." The Assyrians, as was their custom, took the conquered people and scattered them throughout their empire in order to diminish their identity and prevent rebellions. After the destruction of the northern kingdom, the historical books turned to the southern kingdom, with the focus on its capital city, Jerusalem.

The Temple that Solomon had built was destroyed in 586 BCE. Some decades later, by permission of the Persian ruler, it was rebuilt only to be destroyed again in 70 CE by the Romans. The historical books span approximately 600 years, from the establishment of David's kingdom around the year 1000 BCE until the return to Jerusalem under Ezra and Nehemiah in the mid-fifth century BCE.

Even though the "Prophets" section of the Bible is separate from the historical books, we must understand that the prophets lived during the years described in the historical books. The prophets were divided into two categories—the major prophets and the minor prophets. The major prophets included Isaiah, Jeremiah, Ezekiel and Daniel (though in some traditions the latter is viewed as a minor prophet or even as part of the historical books). There were twelve minor prophets as well, in addition to some other prophets who didn't have entire books named after them.

The major theme of the prophets is, in many ways, the major theme of the Bible. The prophets were God's messengers to Israel, calling upon the people to repent, to turn from their rebellious ways and to return to God.

It is incorrect to think that the chief role of prophets was to predict the future. The prophets certainly did predict the future, but even more importantly, they challenged those who were listening to them to participate in God's purpose in changing the present. One of the best illustrations of this is in the Book of Jonah, where the prophet was sent to Nineveh to call upon the Assyrians to repent of their sins. To Jonah's great surprise, they actually did repent, thus averting God's wrath.

The prophets spoke to the present and also described the future. In one sense, the future foreseen by the prophets was assured by God, who is all-powerful. However, because the prophets also spoke to the present and God created and respects human free will, it was clear that humans could change their destiny tomorrow by responding well today.

Unfortunately, the story of the Bible demonstrates that the Jewish people did not often respond as well as one might have hoped. Any other people group would have done the same, as we all have the same forefather and mother in Adam and Eve. But the Lord chose the Jewish people to be the focal point of God's purposes during this period of history.

When we read the Hebrew Scriptures, we recognize that our people are traveling on a spiritual journey. We had a map, we had directions, and there was a voice coming from the heavenly GPS telling us to turn and follow the recalculation to the correct path—but no one listened.

The Bible contains much more material of different types. At the heart of our synagogue worship today are the Psalms, songs of the heart written to God by David and others. Often, they were put to music. The Proverbs, the Song of Solomon and even Lamentations, written by the prophet Jeremiah, are often described as wisdom literature.

One only needs to read through these books of the Bible to see the beauty and wisdom available in them. It would be impossible to read through the Psalms and the wisdom literature without becoming more aware of who God is and who we are as well. The Psalms and wisdom literature tell the same story as the rest of the Bible—that

God loved us and created us for His purposes, but that we failed to respond well to Him, and because of our sin and selfishness we have turned what could have been a pretty happy existence into a world filled with problems and sorrow.

The great hope of the Hebrew Scriptures is the Messiah. At His coming, all of the trouble humankind has brought upon itself through our sin and rebellion would dissipate. This is the hopeful conclusion of the biblical story. The Messiah will come and reign in Jerusalem, ruling not only with an iron rod, as predicted by Isaiah, but also with justice, mercy and peace. The world, tainted by the sin of our first father and mother, will be healed and true *Tikkun Olam* will be manifested on Earth.

It is not easy to summarize the whole story of the Bible in a few sentences—but neither is it that hard. God created a perfect world, including a perfect man and woman, and gave them free will—which was used poorly. Adam and Eve rebelled, as did the generations that followed them. For years and years, God intended use the Jewish people to bring mercy to the world, but His people rebelled. After this, God sent His Messiah to reconcile people to Himself, as predicted by the prophets. One day, the Messiah who died and rose again will return, abolishing the curse and establishing His throne of mercy and justice on Earth.

BIBLICAL ACCURACY: HISTORY, SCIENCE, GEOGRAPHY AND CULTURE

The Bible is not a textbook on history, science, geography or cultural anthropology. It is not designed to give comprehensive information on ancient religions, chronologies or ancient trade routes. Certainly, modern archeology has done more to confirm the historical accuracy of the Hebrew Scriptures than to not cause us to question it. There is no doubt that future researchers will continue to attempt to prove the Bible true based on current scientific theories or comparison with other historical records.

However, proving the accuracy and validity of the Bible is somewhat like proving the existence of God. One can put forth a mountain of evidence—but how do we ultimately determine what is true? Consider the fact that we cannot squeeze God into a scientific method that was intended to describe and measure creation, not the Creator. There are multiple arguments for the validity of the Bible, but what has the weight of evidence to one person does not necessarily have the weight of evidence with another.

I am not diminishing the importance of external verification for the accuracy of the Bible. But ultimately accepting that the Bible is true will involve a combination of faith and objective verification. Sound faith is based on sound facts and there are many facts that establish the accuracy of the Bible. But the Bible is not a comprehensive textbook on science, history or even religion. The Bible is the story of the Jewish people and of God.

If you are of the opinion that the Bible is primarily a collection of myths and stories of an ancient culture— please reconsider. There is a temptation for us to fall into the trap of "modern academic arrogance." In other words, we believe that the past can and should be evaluated on the basis of what we understand and know today.

When this idea is applied to the Bible, we are quick to dismiss its historical accuracy because we approach the Scriptures with a commitment to Western humanism and rationalism, which is in itself a philosophy that colors our view. When imposed on the Scriptures, it provides a faulty matrix for evaluation.

It is not intellectually honest to dismiss the historicity of biblical events—from the parting of the Red Sea to the giving of the Law on Mount Sinai or the nature of predictive prophecy—simply because we have been influenced to believe, without good reason, that the Bible is myth.

In fact, over the last hundred years, far more about the story of Scripture has been proven true than has been proven false. Many of the details in the Bible—the chronology, geography, marriage customs, and more— have been confirmed rather than disproved by the discoveries of ancient artifacts and writings, such as the Dead Sea Scrolls.

In order to understand Isaiah chapter 53 effectively, it might be good to set aside some of the ways in which we tend to prejudge the Bible and instead allow it to speak for itself.

Chapter 3:
Biblical Prophecy—
The Future Unfolds

Prophecy forms a major part of the Bible, and the prophets themselves are very important to the unfolding story of the Hebrew Scriptures. Biblical prophecy goes beyond simply telling the future, for it also includes the prophet's ability to speak God's message to the present.

The Biblical View of Time

The Israelites had a view of time that resonates with most Westerners today. Several of the other ancient cultures had a completely different view of time.

The biblical view of time is linear, whereas in some other cultures it was cyclical or subject to a series of patterns. The story of the Bible, on the other hand, is ever moving forward, giving the reader a sense of progress—as if the entire story were leading towards a point of culmination. According to the Bible, the future event towards which history is headed is the coming of the Messiah and the establishment of the Messianic kingdom. In other words, history will come to a conclusion. This is very different from other cultures that believe history is forever repeating itself and there is no conclusion, just a series of new beginnings.

The prophets could predict the future because of the understanding that time moved from a definite starting point to a definite conclusion. This is the basis for biblical prophecy: the fact that the future is known by God and He uses the prophets to reveal some of what will eventually come to pass. Why? So that when a prophet's predictions came to pass, the Israelites would know that the prophet was a genuine messenger of God. In addition, it meant that the everyday Jewish person of that era could have a sense of hope and confidence in the future—especially during difficult times.

THE FUTURE ACCORDING TO THE BIBLE

The future described by the Bible focuses on three distinct groups. The future of the nation of Israel is perhaps the greatest focus. Second is the focus on the nations of the world—those who are not physical descendants of Abraham, Isaac and Jacob. The third group is that of humans as individuals; the Bible describes our personal futures in many different ways.

The New Testament adds one more group: the community of believers in Yeshua, both Jews and Gentiles (sometimes called the Church), which exists in the days between the first coming of Yeshua and the end of the age. This "end of the age" described in the New Testament is the same as the one described in the Hebrew Scriptures—it is the gateway or bridge into the Messianic kingdom.

You may have heard the famous verse from Isaiah 65:25: *"The wolf and the lamb shall feed together...."* The reason that the wolf (or lion) will lay down with the lamb is because the curse of sin, which came into the world with Adam and Eve, will have been lifted.

Many of the Psalms of King David, who often acted as a prophet, were written to inspire hope—David had a deep sense of where history was ultimately going. Hope always involves the future, and the view of the future according to the Hebrew Scriptures was bright for the faithful. True hope, founded on the Bible, allows us to rise above the present circumstances and challenges of life.

This is not to say that we avoid the present or life's difficulties, but simply that we understand where the story of humanity is heading. Other religions and cultures offer different types of hope. In Hinduism, for example, adherents are told that one day their cycle of incessant reincarnation could end with merging into the one great consciousness—if and when they reach a certain level of personal purification.

One of the great differences between biblical hope and the hope offered by other religious faiths and cultures is that the biblical vision of the future will take place whether we choose to participate or not. The future coming of the Messiah is as sure as the creation of the world. There is nothing that can stop the coming of the Messiah and the coming of His kingdom.

THE NATURE OF PROPHECY

Prophecy can be divided into three categories. Some prophecies are fulfilled immediately—there are many examples of these in the Bible. Other prophecies have an intermediate fulfillment: these are prophecies that would take many years to unfold, but that are not necessarily attached to the "end of the age." Finally, end-time prophecy deals with events that are still in the future.

The fulfillment of immediate and intermediate prophecies confirms the truths of Scripture and of God's plan. We gain hope and the confidence that prophecies of future days will also come to pass, in the same way as the immediate and intermediate prophecies have.

There are many Messianic prophecies in the Bible that have intermediate fulfillment. For example, some prophecies, such as Isaiah 53, were fulfilled by Yeshua in the first century. Other prophecies about the Messiah and His kingdom point to the culmination of God's plan and focus on the events of the end of days.

Prophecies of the destruction of the Temple, the birth of the Messiah, the scattering of Israel from the land and even the return of the Jewish people to the land of Israel are intermediate prophecies. They are not associated with the end of days, but the fact that they have been fulfilled is a massive hint that those prophecies about the end of days will also come to pass.

Fulfilled prophecies—especially those that we've termed intermediate—can be viewed as evidence of the existence of God and the trustworthiness of Scripture. Perhaps even more importantly, fulfilled prophecy shows that God does have a plan for humanity that is working itself out over the course of the years of our lives and will continue during future generations.

The God who told Abram that He would create a nation from his loins and give them a land to live in is the same God who predicted through His prophets that one day our swords will be turned into plowshares (Isaiah 2:4), that the Messiah will reign on David's throne and that there will be no end to the increase of His government (Isaiah 9:6-7). This same God also told us in Isaiah 53 that this Messiah who will someday rule, would first die and rise from the dead.

God, through His prophets, also foretold that an array of nations would try to destroy the Jewish people but that they would not succeed. Through His prophet Jeremiah, God also promised that one day He would make a new covenant with the Jewish people; the old covenant made through Moses at Mount Sinai would be transformed (Jeremiah 31:31).

Do you really believe that it is coincidence that the Jewish people have not only survived repeated attempts to annihilate us, but that God has also brought us back to the very land He promised to us in the Scriptures? If these prophecies have been fulfilled with such accuracy, we may trust that biblical prophecy is accurate and that other prophecies will also come to pass.

PROPHETIC ACCURACY

Moses is the one who set the standards for prophetic accuracy in the Hebrew Scriptures. In Deuteronomy 18:17-22, the lawgiver described the role of prophets and directly addressed the issue of prophetic accuracy. In summary, Moses told us that if a prophecy does not come to pass, then the Israelites would have the right to utilize capital punishment and execute the prophet for his misstatements. Needless to say, that would make a prophet quite cautious in claiming that he was speaking on God's behalf, whether about events in the future or in the present.

Moses himself actually acted as a prophet. In chapter 4 of the fifth Book of the Torah—Deuteronomy or *D'varim,* which was written just prior to the Israelites' entrance into the promised land—Moses predicted that one day the Israelites would be forced out of the land. Later, however, in what he termed "the latter days" (the future Messianic kingdom we described previously), the Jewish people would turn back to God in the lands of the Gentiles and return to the land of Israel.[5]

Later on in Deuteronomy (chapter 28) Moses predicted that the Jewish people would cross the Jordan and enter the land, but because of their disobedience they would be removed.[6] Moses described the years outside the land of Israel as times of great tribulation for the Jewish people, as well as of temptation to worship idols. This is confirmed in a previous chapter in the Book of Leviticus (chapter 26).

Did the Jewish people enter the promised land under the leadership of Joshua? They certainly did! Did the Jewish people eventually find themselves removed from the land of Israel and scattered throughout the nations of the Gentiles because of their disobedience to the Torah? Absolutely! The fulfillment of biblical prophecy is a powerful argument for the trustworthiness of Scripture.

It is fair to ask if the prophecy has been fully fulfilled. Did the Jewish people leave the lands of the Gentiles and return to the land of Israel, repenting and finding themselves restored by God? This is a more difficult claim to make, because the story is not yet over. We can certainly see that, in part, the Jewish people have "miraculously" returned to the land of promise— however, most Israelis are not religious and many are agnostics or atheists. So the part of the prophecy in which our people repent and return to our relationship with God has not yet come to pass.

There is no question that this intermediate prophecy of Moses is accurate. In fact, Ezekiel, whose famous prophecy of the dry bones is written in chapter 37 of the book that bears his name, confirms it. In this instance, we see that the Jewish people are back in the land, but not yet completely restored. In chapters 36 and 37 of the Book of Ezekiel, we see this spiritual transformation taking place in the land of Israel itself.

Since Ezekiel wrote during Israel's exile in Babylon, it is clear that this full restoration and spiritual transformation did not take place then—and has still not taken place. We can conclude that the return of the Jewish people to the land of Israel is a partial fulfillment of prophecy. Since Ezekiel's prophecy shows the Jewish people being restored in stages, it should not surprise us that we have returned to the land without having a dynamic personal relationship with the God of Abraham, Isaac and Jacob. This spiritual renewal was prophesied to occur once our people were back in the land.

MESSIANIC PROPHECY

Our study so far helps us to understand Messianic prophecy. There are two types of Messianic prophecy. The first is intermediate prophecy, which involves the person of the Messiah, His qualifications, the time of His coming and all that He would do when He came. The second type is end-time prophecy, which involves the Messianic age and the culmination of history. In this framework, it becomes obvious that there very well could be two comings of one Messiah—the first coming to accomplish certain tasks, and the second coming linked to the culmination of history.

Some prophecies about the Messiah actually span both first and second comings—both the intermediate and the culmination prophecy. But many are specific to either the first or second coming. It is not always easy to distinguish between them, but the language of the text may provide the answers.

ISAIAH 53 AND THE BIBLE

The chapter under discussion, Isaiah 53, is part of the Hebrew Scriptures. We believe that this passage predicts the accomplishments of Jesus as described in the New Testament more than 700 years later.

If you believe that the Bible is trustworthy, then you can make a rational decision about whether the life and teachings of Jesus fulfill the prophecies of the Hebrew Scriptures—particularly Isaiah chapter 53.

If you are not yet sure what you think about the Bible, take a look at the evidence anyway. If the prophecy in Isaiah 53—with its specificity and historical accuracy—is indeed fulfilled over 700 years later in Yeshua, then that is a pretty good case that both the New Testament and the Hebrew Scriptures are reliable.

I suppose it depends on how you were raised and where you are at this point in your life. I myself was raised with a more traditional view of the Bible, which I did not accept or believe. I was raised in an Orthodox Jewish religious environment and was taught to accept that the

Torah was given by God to Moses at Mount Sinai, and that every word of the *Tanakh* is to be accepted as true, accurate and authoritative. Did I believe this? Absolutely not! It flew against who I was as a freethinker.

However, when I came to see the predictive accuracy of the Hebrew Scriptures—especially Isaiah chapter 53—I became convinced that Yeshua did, in fact, fulfill the prophecy. This led me to reconsider how I felt about my own Hebrew Scriptures. I reopened the question of whether they were accurate, authoritative and should be taken more seriously.

Wherever you are at this moment, try to have an open mind. Then and only then will the prophecy of Isaiah chapter 53 make sense to you.

CHAPTER 4:
THE PROPHET ISAIAH—
HIS MESSAGE AND HIS TIMES

THE ROLE OF THE PROPHET

There are instances in the Hebrew Scriptures where God spoke directly to people, and sometimes He used angels and even donkeys as His messengers. He used visions, dreams and even the mysterious *Urim* and *Thummim,*[7] described in the Book of Exodus, as ways to speak to His people.

God primarily spoke to the Jewish people through the prophets, who were His spokesmen. There were a number of other prophets in addition to the major and minor prophets whose writings are included in the Hebrew Scriptures. Elijah and Elisha were two of the greatest prophets, and they never had books of the Bible of their own. There were also schools of prophets that King Saul encountered on one of his many trips to try to kill David.

The prophets of those days would not be "religious" in our usual sense of the term. They roved the streets, the marketplaces and the countryside, sent by God to a variety of locations in order to speak His word to His people. They were detached from the Temple and never played a particular part of the established religious worship of the day. This is one of the reasons it would be a faulty comparison to think of today's rabbis or ministers as modern-day prophets. Usually a prophet, although respected, stood on the edge of society speaking God's voice into situations that usually demanded correction. As we saw in the previous chapter, they spoke to both the present and the future.

There were also a number of prophets in the New Testament, but none greater than Yohanan haMatbil, also known as John the Baptist. Yeshua Himself said that he was the last great Jewish prophet (Matthew 11). John the Baptist was a surly character who lived in the desert and spoke the truth that God put in his mouth with such passion that ultimately he paid with his life.

Among the prophets we know about from Scripture were farmers, statesmen, common men and women, young prophets like Jeremiah, and older ones. Some of the prophets' lives spanned the reigns of multiple kings in Israel. What they all have in common is that they fearlessly spoke for God (the reluctant Jonah could be an exception!) and usually delivered a challenging message to the Jewish people.

PROPHETS, PRIESTS AND KINGS

In order to have a better idea of how prophets stood within the society, it might be good to take a moment to understand how the Jewish nation was organized and how it operated. The Jewish people were a patriarchal and tribal society before their residence in Egypt, where they spent 400 years—some in slavery.

The Israelite nation began under the leadership of Moses, who filled a role that could be described as a combination of President, Prime Minister, Secretary of State and Chief Justice of the Supreme Court. Moses' brother Aaron was a descendant of Levi, one of the twelve sons of Jacob. Levi's descendants formed a priestly caste whose duties were in the Tabernacle in the wilderness, and later on in the Temple, as it became a more fixed worship center in the heart of Jerusalem.

Moses functioned as a prophet in the truest sense of the word, as he communicated God's messages to the Jewish people. Essentially, prophets spoke for God and priests mediated between man and God (primarily in sacrifice and worship).

God Himself wanted to be Israel's king. But Israel complained about not having an earthly king like the other nations of the world, so God consented and appointed Saul as king. This was unusual, because Saul was from the tribe of Benjamin and not from the tribe of Judah, which according to Genesis 49:10 was to be the progenitor tribe for Israel's rulers and ultimately for the Messianic king.

These three anointed offices—prophet, priest and king—led the Jewish people for years. Sometimes the king turned from the God of Israel and worshiped idols—like King Ahab, for example. But in general, the prophet was the conscience of the king and the ethical backbone of the nation. God spoke to and through the prophets, and the prophets spoke to the kings and to the Jewish people. Eventually, some of what was said was written down on scrolls, which have become our Scriptures.

The prophet was God's voice to the Jewish people regarding the events of the future and the ethical conduct of the present.

Who was the Prophet Isaiah?

Isaiah was a scholar and statesman serving as a prophet under the reign of at least four Jewish kings. He was also a humble man, as is indicated by his call to ministry described in Isaiah chapter 6. Isaiah recognized that he, like his own people, had unclean lips—and he could not make himself holy or righteous. He was overwhelmed by the palpable presence of God and realized his own need to be cleansed from sin. Just then in the vision, an angel lifted a coal from the altar where the daily sacrifices were made and pressed it to Isaiah's lips, symbolically purifying his soul and his message.

The Hebrew language used by Isaiah is some of the most eloquent and lofty language of the Bible. Isaiah was born in a privileged position and functioned as a member of the king's court throughout most of his career. In some ways, Isaiah was not as radical as Jeremiah or Ezekiel, who were called upon by God to do some of the more dramatic and symbolic actions in the Bible.

His work as a prophet began while Uzziah was king.[8] Isaiah seemed very attached to King Uzziah and was probably shaken up by his death—which became the context for his own vision and call to ministry (chapter 6).

He served as prophet under three other Judean kings[9] and just as many Gentile rulers. He was married, had two children whose names were prophetic in character, and his wife was also called a prophetess.

During the first part of Isaiah's ministry, Assyria, which covered an area in Mesopotamia that includes modern-day Iraq, was still the dominant international superpower that regularly threatened the southern kingdom of Israel. Isaiah continually warned the Jewish people against the wiles of the Assyrian leaders, while at the same time calling upon Judah to repent so that God would not allow the Assyrians to destroy them. He had a similar ministry later, after the Babylonians conquered the Assyrians: warning the Israelites to obey the Torah so that the Babylonians would not be brought in by God as a tool of His judgment. Unfortunately, the Jewish people did not repent, and ultimately the Babylonians did attack the Jews and destroy the Temple. These were intermediate prophecies that were fulfilled—which I am sure Isaiah wished would not come to pass.

THE MESSAGE OF ISAIAH

Much of Isaiah's message was a response to the external military threats confronting the southern kingdom and to the moral and ethical threats that came from within. Both the external and internal threats had the capability of bringing certain destruction upon the southern kingdom—which eventually happened with Babylon.

In the Book of Chronicles, the author makes a comment that confirms the preaching of Isaiah, especially as it pertains to the internal threats faced by the Jewish people—even though good kings like Hezekiah and Josiah tried to turn the nation from sin and prevent the coming judgment.[10]

In fully understanding the story of the Bible, it is clear that the internal threat to the nation's well-being because of their disobedience far outweighed the external threat of nations like Babylon that sought to conquer Israel. The message of Isaiah was repentance, and he preached it with passion and urgency for decades because he had seen what had happened to the northern kingdom. He knew why it had been conquered by Assyria, and was doing all he could to keep that from happening to the southern kingdom. This is also one of the reasons why the future Messianic kingdom became such a dominant theme of Isaiah's prophetic message.

Isaiah saw the helplessness of humankind to conquer sin and evil inclinations and to obey God so that they could enjoy individual, personal happiness, as well as national safety and security. Because God's covenant with the Jewish people specified that they would be cast out of the land of promise if they continued to harden their hearts towards God, Isaiah knew that there were tremendous implications to their ongoing sin and rebellion. These themes of judgment, repentance and future hope dominated his prophetic career of almost half a century.

With 66 chapters, the Book of Isaiah is the longest prophetic work in the Hebrew Scriptures. The first 39 chapters emphasize God's judgment on the Jewish people—both the immediate judgment and also the consummate judgment. The last 27 chapters of the Book of Isaiah are mostly future-oriented and primarily focus on the Messiah and His role in the transformation of our sin-cursed planet into a place that can rival and perhaps even surpass the original Garden of Eden.

Isaiah chapters 1 and 5 are difficult to read, as they describe the personal and national sins of the Jewish people. It is interesting to note that the concept of sin is downplayed in some modern understandings of Judaism. Perhaps this is influenced by today's culture, which has toned down the sovereign and transcendent nature of God. Instead we have elevated reason, the material world and our own experience. When sin is measured by standards we establish rather than by standards God established, we will always come out looking less sinful. However, I think we all know deep in our own souls that we most often do not even meet our own standards for righteousness—much less God's.

The message of the Book of Isaiah is highly Messianic in character. There are prophecies that point us to the consummation of the ages—especially chapters 60-66, where the prophet described the future. He presented a vision of a world that has been redeemed, in which the curse of sin has been lifted.

There are also a series of intermediate Messianic prophecies. Some of them speak of the nature and character of the Messiah (9:6-7 and chapter 11) and even His birth: in Isaiah 7:14 we find the controversial prophecy of the virgin birth. The second half of the Book of Isaiah contains the "Servant songs," including Isaiah chapter 53, which describes how Messiah will suffer and die to save the Jewish people as a nation and all people individually.

Isaiah also prophesied about the future of Syria, Iran, Egypt and other nations. His vision of the future describes the relationship between Israel and the nations of the world—which is one of the great challenges of our modern era. According to Isaiah, there will ultimately be peace in the Middle East, but that peace will only come when the Messiah reigns on the earth.

CHAPTER 5:
THE SERVANT OF THE LORD

The prophecy under consideration in this book actually begins with Isaiah 52 verse 13. The passage begins with the phrase, "Behold, my Servant will prosper..." There is no doubt that the main character in the prophecy is the Servant of the Lord, and the more we know about the ancient Hebrew idea of the Servant, the better we will understand the text. Who is this Servant of the Lord? Is it Isaiah? This is very doubtful from the text. Is the Servant to be identified with the nation or corporate Israel? Yes, in some instances, but not in all. Then who else could this Servant of the Lord be?

Identifying the Servant—or Servants, for that matter—is essential to our understanding of Isaiah 53. However, the Servant of the Lord in Isaiah 53 must be understood in light of a number of other passages that are usually called the "Servant songs" in this section of Isaiah.

These "Servant songs" are found in Isaiah chapters 42-61. Scholars throughout the spectrum of biblical interpretation identify two primary possible servants: the Messiah and the nation of Israel. Dr. Walter Kaiser, a Christian scholar who holds a Ph.D. from Brandeis University, explains that the Servant in these passages[11] may refer either to an individual—even a Messianic individual—or to the nation of Israel viewed as a corporate whole.[12]

In the following passages, it seems that the prophet had the entire nation of Israel in mind: Isaiah 41:8 ff., 43:8 ff., 44:26 ff., 48:20. On the other hand, a careful reading of Isaiah 42:1-9, 49:1, 49:5-9 and 52:13-53:12 demonstrates that the references to the Servant of the Lord in these passages are to an individual—likely the Messiah Himself.

Finally, there are a number of passages that could refer to a variety of choices for the Servant of the Lord. These passages are found in Isaiah 49:1, 50:4-11 and 61:1-4.

The identity of the Servant of the Lord—whether the corporate nation of Israel or an individual—is crucial in determining whether or not Yeshua is the fulfillment of the passage. If it can be demonstrated that the Servant of the Lord in Isaiah 53 is an individual and not the nation of Israel, then the case for Yeshua being the fulfillment is far more tenable.

The Servant in the Hebrew Scriptures

The Hebrew word *eved*, used almost 800 times in the Hebrew Scriptures, is translated either as "slave" or "servant." It appears 31 times in Isaiah chapters 40-53, and is often linked with "Lord." According to Dr. Kaiser's research, the title "the Servant of the Lord" is used of significant individuals in the Old Testament such as Moses (17 times), Joshua, David and even Abraham, Isaac and Jacob.[13] The term is used of the prophets as well, and one of the most famous contemporary Jewish books on the subject, written by Abraham Joshua Heschel, is entitled *My Servants the Prophets*.

The word is built upon the Hebrew root *avad*, which is used 290 times in the Hebrew Scriptures. It is commonly understood as one of the terms in the Bible for work. Our rabbis also use the related term *avodah* as one of the words for worship. In this, our sages are telling us that worshiping God may be viewed as hard work.

The *eved Adonai*—the Servant of the Lord—is an individual who carries out the will of God and is totally subservient to his divine master. The background for this idea is worth taking a moment to understand. According to the Torah, an Israelite who fell into debt or lost his land could indenture himself as a servant to a fellow Israelite. However, after six years, he would be released and could buy back his land if possible. Some Israelites actually chose not to leave their service but to further indenture themselves to their master. A special earring was placed in the ear of the servants to indicate that they now served their master voluntarily. Usually, they did this out of gratitude, because they were treated so well during the six years of being indentured to their master.[14]

This helps frame our understanding of the word "servant." The image is that of individuals who willingly serve their master out of love, gratitude and even out of a sense of debt. They have forsaken their own dreams and vision for their lives and submitted themselves to the will of a benevolent master.

CHAPTER 6:
THE SACRIFICE OF THE SERVANT

One of the most difficult concepts to grasp is how the death of someone who lived more than 2,000 years ago impacts individuals today.

The principle of death leading to life occurs regularly in nature. There are many illustrations from nature that point to the necessary death of one thing in order to give life to another. When a seed is planted, it dies in order for a beautiful flower to come into being.

Yeshua Himself used a farming illustration when He spoke about a seed that falls into the ground and dies in order to produce new and greater fruit (John 12:23-26).

We see this principle in the course of human relationships as well. In fact, those willing to sacrifice their own concerns, dreams, careers and finances for the good of others are people we usually admire.

When we hear about a soldier who takes a bullet for another, or covers a land mine with his own body to save someone else's life, we understand that this depth of sacrifice—sacrifice to the point of death—enables others to live.

We also admire immigrants who leave their countries to go to another place to benefit their descendants. This is a very Jewish story, as many Eastern European immigrants came to the United States years ago to provide a better tomorrow for their children. Many brilliant students come to the United States from overseas to improve themselves for the sake of their families and nations, enduring the sacrifice of separation from family and friends.

We all admire a self-sacrificial leader. Though we understand that leadership has its rewards—financially, in increased status, power and influence—we generally admire leaders who work diligently for the benefit of their coworkers and subordinates. We are impressed with a leader who does not take all the perks, stock options or other benefits to which he or she might be entitled, but rather seeks the good of the company and of the people in it.

Historically, leaders who "go without" and sacrifice themselves for the good of others are far more admired than those who hoard wealth for themselves. Warren Buffet is a good example of a business leader who is known for humility and disciplined self-sacrifice. There are many examples in the religious, political and academic realms as well. As for selfish leaders, we may fear them but we do not admire them.

When we speak about the sacrifice of Yeshua, we are speaking about another great leader who was willing to sacrifice Himself for the betterment of those He cared for and served.

The text of Isaiah chapter 53 introduces us to a Servant of the Lord who is not admired for His charismatic personality, good looks, popularity or great wealth:

> *For he shot up right forth as a sapling,*
> *and as a root out of a dry ground;*
> *he had no form nor comeliness,*

that we should look upon him,
nor beauty that we should delight in him. (Isaiah 53:2)

Rather, the person described by the prophet is depicted as marginalized by society and misunderstood.

He was despised, and forsaken of men,
a man of pains, and acquainted with disease,
and as one from whom men hide their face:
he was despised, and we esteemed him not. (Isaiah 53:3)

Yet the Servant exemplifies an extraordinary altruism, and willingly suffers for the benefit of those who reject Him and treat Him poorly. This person is willing to part with His limited worldly possessions, good health, reputation and self-respect for the sake of those who are undeserving and ungrateful.

Surely our diseases he did bear, and our pains he carried;
whereas we did esteem him stricken, smitten of God, and afflicted.
But he was wounded because of our transgressions,
he was crushed because of our iniquities: the chastisement of our
welfare was upon him, and with his stripes we were healed.
All we like sheep did go astray, we turned every one to his
own way; and the LORD hath made to light on him the
iniquity of us all. (Isaiah 53:4-6)

According to Isaiah, the Servant of the Lord somehow bears all the problems and pain we bring upon ourselves that result from living according to our own principles and not God's. This person takes upon Himself the punishment that would otherwise befall us; He receives the judgment brought on by our moral failures.

By oppression and judgment he was taken away,
and with his generation who did reason?

for he was cut off out of the land of the living,
for the transgression of my people
to whom the stroke was due. (Isaiah 53:8)

There is no question that the individual described by the prophet in Isaiah 53 is a Servant hero to men, women, Jews, Gentiles—all humanity!

The chapter teaches that the Servant endured all of the pain, suffering and judgment that you and I should have borne as a result of our ignoring God and living according to our standards and expectations without taking into consideration those of the Creator.

Because He was rejected, we are accepted by God. Because He was alienated from God, we are drawn near to our heavenly father. Because He endured the guilt of moral failure, we are forgiven. Because He experienced intolerable pain, we can be healed. Because He bore our punishment, we will not be judged.

THE MOTIVATION OF THE SERVANT

Though all of us appreciate and admire sacrifice for the good of others, there is no doubt that the greatest act of heroism is to lay down one's life for another person. What would move someone to do this?

Love is the motivating force that has driven some to sacrifice their lives for others. A soldier's love for country, a mother's love for her child and a leader's love for his or her community can make them willing to lay down their own lives for the sake of those they love.

Yeshua Himself spoke to the issue when He said,

> *No one has greater love than a person who lays down his life for his friends. (John 15:13)*

There is no doubt that Yeshua fulfills the description found in Isaiah chapter 53 of a self-sacrificing Servant who was willing to lay down all that He had, including His own life, so that others would benefit from His actions. Even if you are not persuaded that Yeshua is the Messiah of Israel, His self-sacrificing spirit deserves our admiration.

We might be tempted to be cynical and say to ourselves, "Nothing is worth the price of one's own life," but in the depths of our souls, we know that a willingness to die for the greater good is the zenith of self-sacrifice and ennobles all of humanity.

Isaiah's writings in chapter 53 take the question of noble self-sacrifice to a new level. The Servant of the Lord in this chapter is described as one who would willingly suffer for the sins of others. His suffering would be far more than an example of self-sacrificing altruism; rather, His death would, in fact, be linked to God forgiving sin. In other words, the death of the Servant of the Lord would be viewed as redemptive.

Redemption is a term that simply means to be bought out of slavery. The Israelites understood redemption because of the yearly Passover. A lamb, innocent and undeserving of death, was sacrificed so that the firstborn males of the Jewish people could be set free from judgment (redeemed) and the Israelites could leave Egyptian bondage behind for the freedom to be found in the promised land. The meaning of the sacrificial death of the lamb on behalf of the Israelites is perhaps exactly what Isaiah had in mind when he described the death of the Servant on behalf of those who deserved punishment for their sins.

This sacrificial death is described in the following verses in Isaiah 53. Notice the emphasis on the Servant's death on behalf of the sins of others.

> *By oppression and judgment he was taken away,*
> *and with his generation who did reason?*
> *for he was cut off out of the land of the living,*
> *for the transgression of my people to whom the stroke was due.*
> *And they made his grave with the wicked,*
> *and with the rich his tomb; although he had done no violence,*
> *neither was any deceit in his mouth.*
> *Yet it pleased the LORD to crush him by disease;*
> *to see if his soul would offer itself in restitution,*
> *that he might see his seed, prolong his days,*
> *and that the purpose of the LORD*
> *might prosper by his hand. (Isaiah 53:8-10)*

The Servant of the Lord dies in the place of men and women, Jews and Gentiles who have sinned and offended a holy God; we are the ones who actually deserve the penalty of death and alienation from God. But God promised through the prophet to send His Servant to bear the punishment for all people so that we can all be forgiven, no longer subject to penalties for our sin. In one sense, the death of the Servant is the fulfillment of the Passover!

In this light, the interpretation that the Servant is the corporate nation of Israel does not make any sense. After all, how could sinful Israel die on behalf of sinful Israel? It makes the words of the text illogical. This is why so many have come to the conclusion that the Servant is the promised Messiah who will one day reign as king, but must first fulfill this prophecy and die for our sins.

Isaiah 53 is a prophecy of how God would take away the "sin barrier" between Himself and humankind in order to initiate the intimate and personal relationship that He created us to enjoy. How can you have a personal relationship with anyone—mother, father, child, spouse, friend—when there are offenses between you and your beloved? To renew a relationship you must remove the offenses. In the case of man and God, what has created the distance between us is our sin, and until we are forgiven, we will never have the close personal relationship with God that He always intended for us to have. Through the suffering and death of the Servant of the Lord, God Himself acted on our behalf to remove the barrier.

Chapter 7:
Isaiah 53 and Atonement

The idea of atonement is one of the most difficult in the Bible to explain; however, it is also one of the most important of all spiritual truths. It would be impossible to grasp the meaning of Isaiah 53 without examining the meaning of atonement.

Even if a Jewish person never observes the Sabbath, surveys of the modern Jewish community indicate that most Jewish people take a day off work, attend synagogue and do something to acknowledge the Day of Atonement—*Yom Kippur*. But do we really understand what this means? We know it involves forgiving others and being forgiven by God (the one day a year we believe in God—with or without evidence!), but most people would have a difficult time defining and explaining the idea of atonement.

Both Judaism and Christianity have this important teaching in common and are built on this concept, so it is very important for us to understand it! The idea that the Servant dies for our sins cannot be understood without grasping what the Bible teaches about atonement.

Atonement, especially substitutionary atonement, is understandably difficult for the modern mind to grasp, as it is based upon certain presuppositions that are not widely accepted today.

The Presuppositions of Atonement

A Personal God

The first idea essential to the concept of atonement is that there is a personal God who made us, loves us, desires to have a relationship with us and who also holds us accountable for our actions. This personal God is holy and righteous and created beauty, love and all the things we enjoy in this life. He gave us parameters for our behavior so that we do not misuse all the blessings He has given us. But for some reason, no moralist or philosopher has been able adequately to explain why we continually stray from the divine guidelines found in the Bible. Ignoring these guidelines is called sin.

Maybe you have heard these ideas before, but you do not accept this view of the world. You might consider sin to be outdated. Perhaps you might be open to the idea of a personal God, but not one who holds you accountable for failing to live as He designed. Maybe you are searching for spirituality and would like to know how to live a happier life, or how the world in general can become a better and more peaceful place to live.

The existence of a personal Creator is not easy to prove scientifically. British author C.S. Lewis pointed out that God cannot be evaluated by the scientific method, as He is the author of all science.

But if there is no God, are we really comfortable with the idea that there is nothing more to this world than what meets the eye? I believe our human spirit longs for more. Does yours?

And if there is a God, but He is completely impersonal and does not hold us accountable for our actions, then are we ready to concede that there is no such thing as right or wrong, or good and evil?

We can always come back later and take a more in-depth look at the question of God's existence and nature. Atonement cannot be fully explained unless we accept the idea of a personal and holy God, so for the sake of understanding this concept, let's for the moment accept the existence of a personal God as described by the Bible.

WE FIND IT DIFFICULT TO MEET GOD'S STANDARDS

The second presupposition foundational to understanding atonement is that people find it difficult—even impossible—to meet God's standards. The Bible describes this "missing the mark" as sin, and claims that sin is endemic to the human condition—no one is perfect. If sin were not universal, then atonement would be optional or only the worst among us would need it. Rather, according to the Bible and also the Jewish religion, we all need atonement!

In our chapter, Isaiah described sin in verse 6 as following our own way in the manner of sheep. It is an apt picture of our moral condition and tendency to follow the crowd, no matter where it is straying!

> *All we like sheep did go astray,*
> *we turned every one to his own way;*
> *and the LORD has laid on him the iniquity of us all.*
> *(Isaiah 53:6)*

Atonement is based on restoring what is broken and removing the offense so that any disruption in our relationship to God can be healed. Our failure to live according to God's expectations has caused a separation between us and God. Atonement presumes that a better and more harmonious relationship with our Creator is possible, though not without a price!

Jews, Christians and Muslims all believe that humans were created in the image of God. Most would agree that this refers to the spirit, soul or immaterial part of human beings. Morally and ethically, we "look" like God—or at least we did when we were first created. We were designed for a relationship, but find ourselves alienated from our Creator.

This alienation from our Creator throughout human history has seriously impacted who we are and the way we live. The Bible traces everything from natural disasters to world wars and interpersonal conflicts to this break in our relationship with God and our apparent inability to live as He wants us to live. Most people, whether religious or not, would agree that something is wrong with our world. We all hope that a more meaningful existence and a peaceful world is possible.

This alienation expresses itself in numerous ways. Households have experienced the trauma of divorce. Those of us who are parents can reflect on the difficulties and conflicts we have had with our children. We have all known broken relationships with friends, family, and colleagues. In the biblical view of life, these fractured relationships are sure indicators of our personal alienation from God Himself.

This chasm between ourselves and our Creator damages our relationships with others and keeps us from being at peace within ourselves. It would be wonderful to be able to say that we live today in a predominantly happy culture where we have a sense of personal peace and security, but the reality is that many of us are unhappy with our lives. We lack peace in our souls, and that lack of peace stems from our inability to be at peace with God.

The pain of this alienation manifests itself in depression, alcoholism and drug use, workaholism and much more. We are a nation and a culture in pain.

Humanism, the belief that man is innately good, does not help us understand human evil. From the Holocaust to the genocide in Darfur, it is evident that man is capable of not only everyday sins, but also of horrendous evil on a grand scale. Based upon the evidence of history, it would take more faith to believe in man's innate goodness than to believe what the Bible says about man's fall.

Traditional Judaism teaches that men and women have both a good and an evil inclination. We have the ability to make either the right or the wrong decision, but it seems as though humanity's natural inclination is to choose poorly. Being selfish is easy; we have to work at being selfless! As a society, we fall into the same patterns over and over—once one war ends, another begins. For all the advances we have made in technology and other areas, it seems that we are incapable of outgrowing the evil inclination of our human nature.

The Book of Isaiah envisions a day of peace and harmony in society and also in nature, as so much of the trouble that comes upon us is a result of natural disaster and devastation. The Scriptures link man-made evil as well as natural disasters with our separation from God. This is why the prophet speaks of a day when even predators and prey will live together in peace!

> *And the wolf shall dwell with the lamb,*
> *and the leopard shall lie down with the kid;*
> *and the calf and the young lion and the fatling together;*
> *and a little child shall lead them. (Isaiah 11:6)*

In the coming day when the benefits of atonement fill the earth, there will no longer be any war:

> *And He shall judge between the nations,*
> *and shall decide for many peoples;*
> *and they shall beat their swords into plowshares,*
> *and their spears into pruninghooks;*
> *nation shall not lift up sword against nation,*
> *neither shall they learn war any more. (Isaiah 2:4)*

There is much more that could be said, and the above is not intended to persuade, but rather to help us consider the possibility that what the Bible teaches about the nature of man better explains what we know about human behavior. Our failure to live up to God's standards is why we desperately need atonement.

MANY PATHS TO ATONEMENT

There are a variety of ways to look for atonement. Some of us try to find atonement through seeking or earning the forgiveness of others. There's nothing wrong with making amends, and as Jews we know that at least once a year this is a major personal project! But making amends is different from receiving atonement.

We might try to earn atonement by personal sacrifice: volunteering or giving money to philanthropy. These efforts have great merit, but once we stop doing them, our sense of peace wanes, so that we live on a perpetual treadmill, seeking atonement generated by our own efforts. We innately know we need to make atonement for the wrongs we have done, but it is in trying that we experience our deepest sense of failure.

May I ask you to take an honest moment and ask yourself the question, "Am I able to atone for my own sins?"

In the movie *Seven Pounds*, Will Smith creates an elaborate plot by which he would atone for an accident he caused by texting on his BlackBerry while driving. He plans to die in such a way that would enable him to give his organs to worthy individuals. As Will Smith works toward his own atonement, he evaluates the character of those whom his death will benefit. This illustrates the difference between atonement from a biblical point of view and atonement from the human perspective. Because Will Smith felt that he had to *earn* atonement, he offered the gift of his organs to others on the basis of their ability to earn redemption through their good character and efforts.

This is typical of many great world religions. Followers of Hinduism believe they can earn atonement by purifying themselves. This is also somewhat true in Judaism, in which we fulfill the *mitzvot* (commandments) in order to make ourselves worthy of God's mercy, grace and forgiveness.

However, this is quite different from the teachings of the Bible. Atonement—removing the alienation and guilt that keep us from a close personal relationship with our Creator—only comes about when the problem of sin is removed. From the Bible's point of view, no one among us is capable of achieving the depth of repentance that would enable us to meet God's holy standards. Most often, we are barely aware of the ways we fail to live as we were created to live. And if we ourselves are the problem, then how could we possibly be the cure? We need help beyond our ability to help ourselves!

Atonement is a Gift from God

Once we accept the presupposition that there is a personal God, and that we fail to meet His standards, we then come to a third presupposition: atonement begins and ends with God's efforts, and our responsibility is simply to accept what God has accomplished on our behalf. In other words, atonement from the Bible's perspective is an unmerited and unearned gift.

In the biblical story, we must consider the importance of the Temple in Jerusalem (originally built by King Solomon) and the sacrifices that were offered in this Temple. Though seemingly archaic, it might be helpful to try to understand what the Bible is trying to teach.

Whenever ancient Israelites sinned, they were called upon by the Torah to offer a sacrifice in the Temple. But the Lord understood that because of our imperfect nature, we would tend not to know about all our sins and would miss atoning for many! Therefore, one day a year was established—the Day of Atonement or *Yom Kippur*—on which the Israelites could rest in the fact that God would forgive the sins they had missed.

The Hebrew word *kafar*, from which we get *Yom Kippur* (the p and the f are sometimes interchangeable), means "covering." On the Day of Atonement, the sins for which the Israelites had not offered a sacrifice were covered. The High Priest would enter into the Holy of Holies and sprinkle the blood of a bull or a goat on the place over which the presence of God hovered, known as the "mercy seat." The sprinkling of this blood would effect the forgiveness of God and provide atonement for each individual. On the Day of Atonement, God would forgive the sins we never noticed, but that He did. This is a wonderful picture of God's mercy to humanity.

Why the shedding of blood? This is a very difficult question for us to answer in the 21st century, as it sounds so barbaric to us. There is no doubt that the Lord wants us to be kind to all of His creation, but let's consider why God asked the Israelites to sacrifice these animals. A key verse to understanding what the Bible teaches about animal sacrifices is Leviticus *(Vayikra)* 17:11:

> *For the life of the flesh is in the blood; and I have given it*
> *to you upon the altar to make atonement for your souls; for*
> *it is the blood that makes atonement by reason of the life.*

Many books have been written on this passage explaining the importance of blood, but we do not have to read volumes to understand why blood is essential. When there is no blood, there is no life. When blood is tainted with disease, individuals suffer—whether from AIDS, Hepatitis C or leukemia—and tainted blood can easily lead to death. In the Bible, blood is the symbol of that which sustains life. When an animal was slaughtered and its blood was shed, it was understood that the animal was experiencing the price and penalty for sin. The death of the animal was a reminder to the worshiper that sin easily leads to death. It also reminded the Israelites of the Passover, when the blood of the lamb had saved their firstborn sons from death.

The New Testament echoes Leviticus 17:11, as Hebrews 9:22 reads:

> *In fact, according to the Torah, almost everything is purified with blood; indeed, without the shedding of blood there is no forgiveness of sins.*

It is clear that the Bible teaches that the shedding of innocent sacrificial blood was necessary for atonement.

Many world religions use animals for sacrifice. This does not make the Bible wrong or right, but it is clear that there have been other faiths in which people have believed that the shedding of blood led to atonement. It is interesting that God spared the life of Isaac when his father, Abraham, was willing to sacrifice him. This demonstrates that the Bible is opposed to human sacrifice, which was a practice allowed by other ancient religions.

There is one instance in the Bible, however, where the Lord does say that He will allow for some type of human self-sacrifice. This is found in Isaiah chapter 53, and we believe it was fulfilled through the death of Yeshua the Messiah. We will soon look at this chapter in relation to Yeshua and ask the question, "Did Yeshua die an atoning death for sin?"

The prophet indicates that the Servant will die as a substitute for us; through His death our sins are forgiven and we are granted the gift of atonement.

Yet it pleased the LORD to crush him by disease;
to see <u>if his soul would offer itself in restitution,</u>
that he might see his seed, prolong his days,
and that the purpose of the LORD might prosper by his hand:
Of the travail of his soul he shall see to the full,
even My servant, who by his knowledge did
justify the Righteous One to the many,
<u>and their iniquities he did bear.</u> (Isaiah 53:10-11)

CONCLUSION

I realize that it is not easy as 21st-century Westerners to comprehend, let alone accept, the biblical view of atonement. First of all, we need to believe that God exists and that He is personal and holy. Second, we need to accept that human beings are incapable of earning atonement on our own. Finally, we must accept that God provides atonement for us through sacrifice and the shedding of blood. These three principles form the basis for our understanding that the Servant in Isaiah chapter 53 died a sacrificial death in order to atone for the nation of Israel and for all the peoples of the earth.

Perhaps you do not accept one or more of these presuppositions. We have been raised to reject these ideas. You might feel as if you have to "park" your brain and accept it all by faith. However, let me suggest that when it comes to the problem of evil, human suffering and our lack of peace, these presuppositions explain our experience just as well—if not better than—the alternatives we commonly accept despite the lack of objective evidence.

Could we really make an airtight case for the innate goodness of humankind in light of what is happening in Afghanistan, Iraq, the Israeli/Palestinian conflict, Sudan, Darfur, North Korea…and what happened on 9/11? We face issues like poverty, racism, antisemitism, global warming and the unmitigated human greed we have witnessed over the last few years in North America and Europe. It sometimes seems to me that the common way we deal with uncomfortable questions regarding human nature and issues of good and evil is by burying our heads in entertainment, video games and other escapes that keep us from facing the real issues of life. So many of us have given up our ideals and are no longer inspired to try to make the world a better place.

What are some alternatives to the biblical view of the world? We once believed that education would bring enlightenment. Has it? Certainly in many areas this might be true, but has further education really given you personal peace and kept you from personal pain and broken relationships? Has education enabled the nations of the world to live in peace?

Has science solved our problems? Perhaps we live longer and more comfortably, but ultimately we still face death. Through science, we can make death more palatable and more comfortable, but has science actually solved the deepest problems of our souls? Certainly it has not.

Think about the beliefs we commonly accept without questioning, and compare them to the biblical solution for personal peace. If what you have tried has worked for you, then maybe believing that Yeshua is the Messiah and has cleared the path for you to have a relationship with your Creator is unnecessary.

But maybe you are still searching. I believe you will discover that "self-help" will be trumped by atonement.

Only through accepting God's atonement will we experience peace in our relationship with our Creator—a peace that will enable us to face life and even death with a confidence that comes from an intimate relationship with the God who made us.

The prophet Isaiah described a future day when we as individuals will enjoy the full blessings of atonement:

> *The spirit of the Lord GOD is upon me; because the LORD has anointed me to bring good tidings to the humble; He has sent me to bind up the broken-hearted, to proclaim liberty to the captives, and the opening of the eyes to them that are bound; To proclaim the year of the LORD's good pleasure, and the day of vengeance of our God; to comfort all that mourn; To appoint unto them that mourn in Zion, to give to them a garland for ashes, the oil of joy for mourning, the mantle of praise for the spirit of heaviness; that they might be called terebinths of righteousness, the planting of the LORD, wherein He might glory. (Isaiah 61:1-3)*

Yeshua Himself quotes from this passage in the New Testament in describing the true *Y'mei Mashiach* (Days of Messiah).

I think that most of us would agree that although there is great beauty and goodness in the world, our cosmos itself is morally and spiritually shattered. Atonement is designed to bring things back together and to restore the "*shalom*" of humanity.

CHAPTER 8:
THE CREDIBILITY OF THE
NEW TESTAMENT

In order to make a solid case that Yeshua is the fulfillment of Isaiah 53, we must examine the authenticity of the information we have about Him. The primary source that describes the life and times of Yeshua the Messiah is the New Testament. The New Testament is not well known outside of the Christian community and is not often read by Jewish people, though it was primarily penned by Jewish writers.

Many different types of literature are included in the New Testament. The four Gospels present us with an historical account of Yeshua's life, and the Book of Acts records the history of the early believers in Yeshua. The various letters of the Apostles are primarily "pastoral" and instructional in nature, and the Book of Revelation is an apocalyptic letter that is similar in style to the books of Ezekiel, Daniel and even parts of Isaiah.

There are many good reasons for trusting the historical credibility of the New Testament records. Once we establish the reliability of these texts, then we can compare the facts of Yeshua's life with the prophecy in Isaiah 53.

It is common to separate the evidence into two distinct categories: internal and external. Because there are so many excellent works on these topics, our comments will be brief.[15]

Internal Evidence

Consistency with the Rest of Scripture

The New Testament is consistent with the Hebrew Scriptures. The focus of the New Testament is still the Jewish people, the setting is still the land of Israel, and the book most often quoted in the New Testament is the Old Testament. The New Testament would not make any sense without understanding the Old Testament concepts of the holiness of God, human sin, and atonement. There is also a great hope for a future Messianic age of world peace.

The New Testament is also consistent with itself. The major focus in the New Testament is the fact that Yeshua is the Messiah and that forgiveness of sins and a personal relationship with God should be the paramount concern of humankind. The basic details about the life, death, resurrection and teaching of Yeshua are consistent between the four Gospels and the remainder of the New Testament. There are certainly complementary teachings and expansions of various ideas and parables, but it is evident that the themes, character and theology are consistent throughout the New Testament.

It is also important to add that the Jewish calendar is prominent in both Testaments. One could easily argue for the Jewishness of the New Testament based upon the calendar, the keeping of the festivals and the way in which Jewish tradition and life are essential to its theology and teaching. So many of the events of Yeshua's life and teachings occur within the framework of the Jewish festivals.

By reading the Bible for yourself, you can make up your own mind as to whether or not these two books are, in fact, one story.

COMPLEMENTARY NOT CONTRADICTORY

Some claim that the Gospels contradict themselves, and some suggest that the teaching of Paul in the New Testament is contradictory with that of James, another important leader in the early community of Jewish believers in Yeshua. However, these writers were not inconsistent, but rather complementary of one another.

There are many examples of this, but one that stands out is the account of the "feeding of the 5,000." This occasion is described in all four of the Gospels, and each telling of the story is a little different from the others. There is also another story in the New Testament of the feeding of 4,000, but this is a separate event.

If one reads through the accounts,[16] it will become clear that there is nothing contradictory when the stories are compared with each other. Each writer fills in a little more information from his own perspective. For example, Mark literally adds some color to the story, as he notes that the grass upon which the people sat down was green. Although the other Gospel writers do not include this detail, one cannot really make a case for "contradictory Gospels" simply because one of the writers mentioned the fact that the grass was green.

There are many other illustrations of the complementary—but not contradictory—perspectives of the four Gospels. The Books of Matthew, Mark and Luke are called the three "synoptic Gospels" (synoptic comes

from a Greek word which means "to see together").
The Book of John is written in a very different style and
focuses far more on the teaching of Yeshua than on His
actions. But there is nothing in the Gospel of John that
contradicts the story of the feeding of the 5,000 in the
other Gospels.

This is simply an illustration of how the process of
inspiration works: each of the Gospel writers, inspired
by the Holy Spirit, presented the life of Yeshua through
his own eyes and personality. Understanding the
Gospels as complementary can solve most of the alleged
"contradictions." They are remarkably consistent in their
fact and their teachings.

We can apply this same principle to the New Testament
as a whole. Did Yeshua, Paul and James really disagree
with each other? All three teach about the necessity of
living by faith, and that it is through faith in Yeshua the
Messiah that we receive forgiveness for sin and the gift
of everlasting life. This faith is not merely an abstract
intellectual "belief"—rather, it is lived out with good
works. Our good works by themselves, however, cannot
provide atonement for us without faith in Yeshua, the
Servant who died a sacrificial death as predicted in Isaiah
53. The New Testament writers may present things from
a variety of angles, but they teach the same truth.

DETERMINING REASONABLE CONTENT
AND "BIBLICAL" QUALITY

There is no doubt that a number of the books that did
not make it into the New Testament canon (a word
which means ruler; i.e. to measure as one would to create
a standard) are becoming more and more popular today.

A few examples are the Gospel of Thomas, the Gospel of Judas and a number of other esoteric documents that tell a different story than those understood to be authoritative by the early Christians and accepted into the canon.

Upon reading some of these extra-biblical documents, it becomes evident that they fall considerably short in the quality as well as the reasonableness of the text. In addition, most of these "alternative Gospels" and other documents—most of which were written later than the New Testament books—are not consistent with the teachings of the Old or New Testaments.

CLAIMS OF THE GOSPEL WRITERS THEMSELVES

The Gospel writers claim that they were either writing well-researched history or were personally involved with Yeshua and were writing about what they experienced. Perhaps the clearest illustration of this is found in the Gospel of Luke:

> *Inasmuch as many have taken in hand to set in order a narrative of those things which have been fulfilled among us, just as those who from the beginning were eyewitnesses and ministers of the word delivered them to us, it seemed good to me also, having had perfect understanding of all things from the very first, to write to you an orderly account, most excellent Theophilus. (Luke 1:1-3)*

Luke was a doctor who traveled with the Apostle Paul. It is evident that he was a man of science, and he did his homework in developing a careful account of Yeshua's life. Luke followed the same methodology in writing the Book of Acts, where he continued the story of Yeshua after His resurrection and recorded the history of the early Jewish and Gentile believers. The reference to the "former account" is obviously the Gospel of Luke:

> *The former account I made, O Theophilus, of all that Yeshua began both to do and teach, until the day in which He was taken up, after He through the Holy Spirit had given commandments to the Apostles whom He had chosen, to whom He also presented Himself alive after His suffering by many infallible proofs, being seen by them during forty days and speaking of the things pertaining to the kingdom of God. (Acts 1:1-3)* [17]

One can argue that eyewitnesses to events are not necessarily good writers of history. You might say that even though Luke claimed to use an adequate historical method to develop a chronological history of Yeshua's life, he still could be inaccurate. However, both of these suppositions would have to be proven, and that is not an easy task—after all, none of us were there to see the events for ourselves!

We know that in Jewish tradition, memory was cherished and nurtured—especially when it came to matters of religion and faith. Jewish people understand that the Scriptures themselves were handed down in an oral format for centuries, as was Jewish tradition. The *Mishnah* (Oral Law) did not begin to reach written form until the early third century CE. Finding value in oral tradition and believing that there was consistency between that oral tradition and what was eventually recorded is not foreign to Jewish faith and practice, nor to many of the great world faith communities of our day.

The Gospel writers appealed to their personal experiences with Yeshua in order to prove the validity of their Gospels. They never felt a particular need to defend their position, because they knew that what they wrote about was true—since they had experienced it.

As the Apostle John wrote,

> *That which was from the beginning, which we have heard, which we have seen with our eyes, which we have looked upon, and our hands have handled, concerning the Word of life—the life was manifested, and we have seen, and bear witness, and declare to you that eternal life which was with the Father and was manifested to us—that which we have seen and heard we declare to you, that you also may have fellowship with us; and truly our fellowship is with the Father and with His Son Yeshua the Messiah. And these things we write to you that your joy may be full. (1 John 1:1-4)*

John unquestionably believed that what he was writing was true, and just because these words were penned many years ago does not mean we can simply dismiss or distrust them because they are old. If we did this, then we would have to doubt almost anything that was ever written in a historical document.

CLOSENESS IN TIME TO THE EVENTS

Since at least three of the four Gospel writers were close associates of Yeshua, they would have written the Gospels very close to the time of Yeshua's life. Virtually all scholars today, even those that are the most critical of the New Testament documents, believe that the Gospels were written within the first century CE.

Many of the "church fathers"—the teachers of the church who lived within two centuries of the life and death of Yeshua—quoted from the Gospels, which evidently meant that they were in existence at the time; and some of these church fathers wrote in the latter part of the first century CE.

The New Testament was formalized at the Council of Nicea in 325 CE, but it is a mistake to think that the documents themselves were not readily available and their historicity accepted by the majority of believers in Jesus in the years prior to the Council. Nicea simply confirmed what believers across the ancient world already knew: the four Gospels and the remainder of the New Testament, from the Book of Acts to the Book of Revelation, were all in regular use by believers. There were probably a limited number of copies, and much of what is contained in the Gospels was likely put to memory by the early believers. This would have been true of the Hebrew Scriptures as well.

In summary, the internal evidence is strong indicating that the New Testament documents were written by those who saw the events of Yeshua's life and wrote in a timely fashion, so that the words of Yeshua and the stories of His life are reliable.

EXTERNAL EVIDENCE

CONTEMPORARY HISTORIANS

The New Testament records, especially the Gospels, should be evaluated as we do the writings of historians living and writing in this same period. The question we might ask is whether we have any more reason to suspect a lack of credibility on the part of the New Testament writers than we might have in reading their Jewish and Gentile contemporaries. Caesar, Livy, Tacitus, Josephus and Herodotus, all of whom wrote within three or four centuries of the New Testament writers, should be judged by the same principles as the authors of the Gospels. The books of the Maccabees and other Jewish literature of a historical nature should be evaluated the same way.

Without initiating a complete study of classical texts, we can say that whatever principles apply to some of these documents should apply to all. For example, Josephus was a Jewish general who became a traitor and joined the side of the Romans during the series of battles that resulted in the destruction of Jerusalem and the Temple. His historical tome, *The Wars of the Jews,* is considered by most to be fairly accurate history. His bias was certainly clear, yet he is respected as someone who wrote a careful history of the period.

The same is true of the authors of the New Testament, particularly the Gospels. These authors, who wanted to share what they knew about Yeshua's life and teaching, should be taken at least as seriously as Josephus.

Contemporary historians have confirmed the geography as well as the social and religious structures of the period described in the New Testament. The marriage and social customs, common religious beliefs and even information about agricultural methods have been verified. No one seriously disputes the dates, the names of Herod or the High Priests or the details of how the Jewish festivals were celebrated at that time.

That leaves the religious aspects of the New Testament documents as the core of any disputes about historical accuracy. The very least we could say about the credibility of the New Testament is that the Gospel writers truly believed what they wrote. They did believe that Yeshua was the Messiah, that He died and that He rose from the dead. They also believed He is going to return one day in His second coming. All of these matters of faith are embedded in the same historical accounts that have been proven accurate in many other areas—so what logical reason do we have to doubt them?

We have to admit that it is primarily our anti-supernatural bias—or even our bias against Jesus being the Messiah—that causes us to consider the New Testament to be "non-historical." We need to reexamine why we do not take the New Testament seriously, and if we cannot find good reason to do so, then we at least need to accept that what the writers reported about Yeshua was as accurate as any other document written at the time. If we choose not to believe that Yeshua did miracles, forgave sin or rose from the dead, then we do so because we simply do not believe these things can happen, not because the facts are misreported.

In other words, the New Testament is good history, and if for some reason a person believes it is "bad religion," then the reason for believing this cannot and should not be based on alleged lack of historical accuracy. We have every good reason to believe that the New Testament writers reported accurately what they knew about the life of Yeshua.

British author Hugh Schonfield believed that the writers of the New Testament, in a conspiracy with the disciples, fabricated the story that Jesus fulfilled the prophecies of the Messiah written in the Old Testament. But why? Did Schonfield have historical and factual reasons to believe that Yeshua did not die, but rather "swooned?"

When one studies Schonfield's life, it is interesting to note that at one time he was a follower of Yeshua, but later rejected Him. It appears that Schonfield was aggressively providing his own reasons for why he denied that Yeshua was the Messiah after having been a believer for many years. We cannot know the intentions of a man's heart, and perhaps Schonfield should have applied the principle of historical objectivity to his own work before accusing the disciples and followers of Yeshua of such deception.

In order to be intellectually honest, we need objective reasons to deny the historicity of the Gospels. Until then, we should compare the life of Yeshua with the prophecy of Isaiah 53 to see if the facts of His life and death match the details in the prophecy. If they do, then we should consider that He just might be the Messiah of Israel.

EARLY CHRISTIAN HISTORY

There are some statements recorded about Yeshua in the Talmud. For the most part, these statements are not complimentary, but they do indicate that there were many in the Jewish community at the time who recognized Yeshua as an historical figure.

There is one Talmudic story that describes an individual who was facing death and was healed by disciples of

Yeshua. The epilogue to the story is not very positive, however, for when the individual heard in whose name he was healed, he is said to have wished that he was still ill!

This is understandable, however, when we consider the history of the Talmud. These traditions were passed down orally, but were not written down until hundreds of years after the time of Yeshua. The *Mishnah* is commonly understood to have been compiled in the third century CE. By that time, there was already considerable tension between the emerging church—which had become primarily Gentile—and the traditional Jewish community, which was about to lose the religious and political "upper hand" to the church during the time of Constantine.

During the first two centuries of "Christian history," when there was still a strong Jewish influence in various sectors of the emerging church, the documents of the New Testament were already well known and treated as historical fact. The early church fathers, especially those who wrote before the Council of Nicea in 325 CE, accepted the New Testament records—particularly the Gospels—as accurate history. In fact, they quoted so often from these texts that if we were to lose every copy of the New Testament in existence today, we would still be able to reconstruct the entirety of the documents from the writings of the church fathers.

The fact that the church fathers quoted extensively from the New Testament documents does not prove their accuracy, but it does tell us that those individuals trusted what was written enough to base their very lives on the veracity and accuracy of these documents. These were the people who had the most at stake, as a number of them became martyrs for their faith. The early church fathers lived not very many years after Yeshua, and some of the first-generation Apostles were still alive, so they would have been more aware of any disputes over the facts in the New Testament. We are aware of some very minor disputes, but none regarding the accuracy of the facts about Yeshua's life.

Of course the above does not "prove" that the documents are reliable, but it strongly suggests that those people who were probably the most concerned with the accuracy of the documents did believe that they were true.

COMPARISONS WITH OTHER DOCUMENTS

The time differences between many events recorded by ancient authors and the manuscripts that we have available today show that the New Testament documents, when compared to other ancient documents, are in fact more credible than most.[18]

CONCLUSION

It has not been our intent to prove that the New Testament is true, but simply to demonstrate that it should not be easily dismissed as flawed history.

There is always an element of faith involved in believing that the Bible is accurate and reliable, as these books are filled not only with matters of history—which can be objectively verified—but also with spiritual issues, which cannot be proven in the same way.

The question we have tried to address is whether or not there is enough evidence to base our faith upon what is contained in both Testaments. Intelligent and thinking people cannot and should not simply dismiss the New Testament—or the Bible as a whole—as fables, stories and myths without good reason. We do not treat other ancient documents in the same way, yet why do some easily dismiss the records of the Bible without sound logical and historical reasons?

To respond to this question honestly, we must try to sort through our personal prejudices. Perhaps we have an emotional reaction to the New Testament, especially if we are Jewish, as classical Christianity is often viewed as historically hostile to the Jewish community. It might also be because we have an anti-supernatural bias and do not believe that God could use men and women to write books that have religious authority. Perhaps we simply doubt the existence of God or have trouble believing that the Lord of the universe wants to communicate His plan and purposes to humankind.

This is all understandable; however, if we consider ourselves to be fair and reasonable, then we really do need better reasons if we are to dismiss the claims of the Bible.

Even if you do not completely accept the credibility of the New Testament, you would still do well to read on as we compare the prophecy in Isaiah chapter 53 with the New Testament Scriptures. It is possible that after a careful examination of the way in which Yeshua fulfills Isaiah 53, you might look at the Scriptures in a new way.

Before we conclude this brief section, can we take an honest look at the very idea of faith? If you think about it, we exercise faith far more than we care to admit. For example, if you are an atheist or agnostic, do you have hard evidence for your position or do you simply accept these ideas without proof? Do you dismiss the idea of Jesus being the Messiah because of the facts of the case or because of the way you were raised? You see, most of us actually base our personal beliefs upon limited facts and lots of faith—but faith built upon limited facts is often faulty. Also, faith can easily be confused with emotion or even prejudice.

Your beliefs may be based upon your emotions or on your religious background, but is this really adequate? You do not make other important life decisions based purely on emotion, without researching the facts. Sound faith is based upon sound facts. So let's take a look at the possibility of Jesus being the Messiah and fulfilling the prophecy in Isaiah chapter 53. What have you got to lose?

CHAPTER 9:
DOES YESHUA FULFILL
ISAIAH 53?

Now that we have provided some background to
the prophecy and have demonstrated that the New
Testament Scriptures may be viewed as accurate history,
it is time to compare both Testaments to see if Yeshua
fulfilled the prophecy. Yeshua Himself did this when,
according to the Gospel writer Luke, He ran into two
despondent disciples after His resurrection.

He walked with them for some time and then opened
their eyes to see who He really was. He then showed
how He fulfilled the prophecies of Messiah's first
coming in the Hebrew Scriptures:

> *Then He said to them, "O foolish ones, and slow of heart to
> believe in all that the prophets have spoken! Ought not the
> Messiah to have suffered these things and to enter into His
> glory?" And beginning at Moses and all the Prophets, He
> expounded to them in all the Scriptures the things concerning
> Him. (Luke 24:25-27)*

We will now take the same approach as we look at the text
of Isaiah 53 in more detail and compare it with the New
Testament Scriptures to answer the question, "Does Yeshua
fulfill the prophecy of Isaiah chapter 53?"

We will attempt to answer this question by comparing

Isaiah's prophecy with the story of Yeshua as described in the first-hand accounts of the disciples who knew Him and who penned the Gospels.

We will begin by dividing the content of Isaiah 53 into two component parts. First, we will look at the description of the Servant's person and character. Secondly, we will review His accomplishments in life and death to see if these are consistent with Yeshua's actions.

THE CHARACTER OF THE SERVANT

In Isaiah 53, the character of the Servant is described in terms of His suffering. Our true character comes out when we are facing difficult or impossible circumstances. This is exactly what the Servant is facing in this chapter, when His character is raw, honest and fully exposed.

Let's look at five aspects of the Servant's character as revealed in Isaiah, compared with what the New Testament Scriptures say about Yeshua.

∞ THE PROPHETIC DESCRIPTION

The Servant was humble:

> *Behold, My servant shall prosper,*
> *he shall be exalted and lifted up,*
> *and shall be very high. (Isaiah 52:13)*

> *For he shot up right forth as a sapling,*
> *and as a root out of a dry ground;*
> *he had no form nor comeliness,*
> *that we should look upon him,*
> *nor beauty that we should delight in him. (Isaiah 53:2)*

The Gospel writers and Peter, speaking in the Book of Acts, describe the way in which Yeshua can be viewed as God's Servant, emphasizing His humility and unselfishness.

> *For even the Son of Man did not come to be served, but to serve, and to give His life a ransom for many. (Mark 10:45)*

> *The God of Abraham, Isaac, and Jacob, the God of our fathers, glorified His Servant Yeshua, whom you delivered up and denied in the presence of Pilate, when he was determined to let Him go. (Acts 3:13)*

> *To you first, God, having raised up His Servant Yeshua, sent Him to bless you, in turning away every one of you from your iniquities. (Acts 3:26)*

Around thirty years after Yeshua's death and resurrection, the Apostle Paul wrote a more theological interpretation of His life and death. Paul spoke to the early believers and encouraged them to serve one another, using the example of Yeshua to make his point:

> *Let this mind be in you, which was also in Messiah Yeshua, Who, being in the form of God, did not consider it robbery to be equal with God, but made Himself of no reputation, taking the form of a bondservant, and coming in the likeness of men. And being found in appearance as a man, He humbled Himself and became obedient to the point of death, even the death of the cross. (Philippians 2:5-8)*

The Servant was willing to suffer the rejection of His community:

> *He was despised, and forsaken of men,*
> *a man of pains, and acquainted with disease,*
> *and as one from whom men hide their face:*
> *he was despised, and we esteemed him not. (Isaiah 53:3)*

Yeshua had human feelings and concerns. Like any of us, He enjoyed acceptance, especially from His own community, the Jewish people. He was willing to give up all of this for the sake of fulfilling the prophecy, which predicted that the Servant would be scorned and ostracized from His people.

∞ THE NEW TESTAMENT FULFILLMENT

The writers of the Gospels make it clear that Yeshua fulfilled these elements of Isaiah's prophecy and endured rejection for our sake.

> *And He began to teach them that the Son of Man must suffer many things, and be rejected by the elders and chief priests and scribes, and be killed, and after three days rise again. (Mark 8:31)*

> *He came to His own, and His own did not receive Him. But as many as received Him, to them He gave the right to become children of God, to those who believe in His name: who were born, not of blood, nor of the will of the flesh, nor of the will of man, but of God. And the Word became flesh and dwelt among us, and we beheld His glory, the glory as of the only begotten of the Father, full of grace and truth. (John 1:11-14)*

The Servant suffered silently and did not retaliate:

He was oppressed, though he humbled himself
and opened not his mouth;
as a lamb that is led to the slaughter,
and as a sheep that before her shearers is dumb;
yea, he opened not his mouth. (Isaiah 53:7)

Revenge and retaliation are normal human responses when we are attacked. The Servant was injured both physically and emotionally, but He was a willing sufferer, showing His excellent character.

∞ THE NEW TESTAMENT FULFILLMENT

The New Testament writers penned a considerable amount about the sufferings of Yeshua. The following is just a sampling of what they observed and chronicled:

And while He was being accused by the chief priests and elders, He answered nothing. Then Pilate said to Him, "Do You not hear how many things they testify against You?" But He answered him not one word, so that the governor marveled greatly. (Matthew 27:12-14)

For to this you were called, because Messiah also suffered for us, leaving us an example, that you should follow His steps: "Who committed no sin, nor was deceit found in His mouth"; who, when He was reviled, did not revile in return; when He suffered, He did not threaten, but committed Himself to Him who judges righteously..." (1 Peter 2:21-23)

The Servant was willing to suffer a sacrificial and humiliating death for the sake of God's people:

> *By oppression and judgment he was taken away,*
> *and with his generation who did reason?*
> *for he was cut off out of the land of the living,*
> *for the transgression of my people to whom the stroke was*
> *due. (Isaiah 53:8)*

Here again we see the impossibility of the Servant in Isaiah 53 being the entire nation of Israel. How can Israel be "cut off" for Israel? Rather, the prophet has an individual in mind, the Servant of God who suffers a humiliating death on behalf of His people—the Jewish people. The only question we must ask ourselves is, "Who is this Servant?"

∞ The New Testament Fulfillment

Isaiah predicted that the Servant would suffer and die sacrificially for us, even though the people on whose behalf He was suffering were rejecting and abusing Him:

> *Then Pilate took Yeshua and scourged Him. And the*
> *soldiers twisted a crown of thorns and put it on His head,*
> *and they put on Him a purple robe. Then they said,*
> *"Hail, King of the Jews!" And they struck Him with*
> *their hands. Pilate then went out again, and said to them,*
> *"Behold, I am bringing Him out to you, that you may*
> *know that I find no fault in Him." Then Yeshua came*
> *out, wearing the crown of thorns and the purple robe. And*
> *Pilate said to them, "Behold the Man!" (John 19:1-5)*

Then the soldiers of the governor took Yeshua into the
Praetorium and gathered the whole garrison around Him.
And they stripped Him and put a scarlet robe on Him. When
they had twisted a crown of thorns, they put it on His head,
and a reed in His right hand. And they bowed the knee
before Him and mocked Him, saying, "Hail, King of the
Jews!" Then they spat on Him, and took the reed and struck
Him on the head. And when they had mocked Him, they
took the robe off Him, put His own clothes on Him, and led
Him away to be crucified. Now as they came out, they found
a man of Cyrene, Simon by name. Him they compelled to
bear His cross. And when they had come to a place called
Golgotha, that is to say, Place of a Skull, they gave Him sour
wine mingled with gall to drink. But when He had tasted it,
He would not drink. Then they crucified Him, and divided
His garments, casting lots, that it might be fulfilled which was
spoken by the prophet: "They divided My garments among
them, And for My clothing they cast lots." Sitting down, they
kept watch over Him there. And they put up over His head
the accusation written against Him: THIS IS JESUS THE
KING OF THE JEWS. (Matthew 27:27-37)

∽ THE PROPHETIC DESCRIPTION

The Servant was a righteous and good man who
suffered innocently:

> *And they made his grave with the wicked,*
> *and with the rich his tomb; although he had done no violence,*
> *neither was any deceit in his mouth.*
> *Yet it pleased the LORD to crush him by disease;*
> *to see if his soul would offer itself in restitution,*
> *that he might see his seed, prolong his days,*
> *and that the purpose of the LORD might prosper by his hand.*
> *(Isaiah 53:9-10)*

Isaiah described the Servant as one who would suffer undeservedly; He was innocent and we are guilty. He endured all that we deserve as a result of our sin although He had lived a perfect life. Like the sacrifices in the ancient Temple, the Servant was without blemish, as He could not have been a proper substitute for us if He were not.

∞ THE NEW TESTAMENT FULFILLMENT

The Gospel writers confirmed the specifics of what was predicted by the prophet as well:

> *Now when evening had come, there came a rich man from Arimathea, named Joseph, who himself had also become a disciple of Yeshua. This man went to Pilate and asked for the body of Yeshua. Then Pilate commanded the body to be given to him. When Joseph had taken the body, he wrapped it in a clean linen cloth, and laid it in his new tomb which he had hewn out of the rock; and he rolled a large stone against the door of the tomb, and departed. (Matthew 27:57-60)*

Peter described the innocence of Yeshua the Messiah:

> *For to this you were called, because Messiah also suffered for us, leaving us an example, that you should follow His steps: "Who committed no sin, Nor was deceit found in His mouth"; who, when He was reviled, did not revile in return; when He suffered, He did not threaten, but committed Himself to Him who judges righteously... (1 Peter 2:21-23)*

Rabbi Saul also added his commentary on the character of the Messiah, based upon Isaiah 53 and the way in which Yeshua lived His life:

For He made Him who knew no sin to be sin for us, that we might become the righteousness of God in Him. (2 Corinthians 5:21)

THE ACCOMPLISHMENTS OF THE SERVANT

Now let's take a brief look at the accomplishments of the Servant according to Isaiah, with a corresponding passage from the New Testament.

∞ THE PROPHETIC DESCRIPTION

The Servant bore our sorrows, grief and sicknesses:

Surely our diseases he did bear,
and our pains he carried;
whereas we did esteem him stricken,
smitten of God, and afflicted. (Isaiah 53:4)

What the Servant would do for us, according to Isaiah, would be very personal and profound. This individual would actually remove our sin and our alienation from God, allowing us to experience the benefits of knowing God personally. The Servant would take away our pains and sorrows, giving us new life and true *shalom*.

∞ THE NEW TESTAMENT FULFILLMENT

Come to Me, all you who labor and are heavy laden, and I will give you rest. Take My yoke upon you and learn from Me, for I am gentle and lowly in heart, and you will find rest for your souls. For My yoke is easy and My burden is light. (Matthew 11:28-30)

...But also for us. It shall be imputed to us who believe in Him who raised up Yeshua our Lord from the dead, who was delivered up because of our offenses, and was raised because of our justification. Therefore, having been justified by faith, we have peace with God through our Lord Yeshua the Messiah, through whom also we have access by faith into this grace in which we stand, and rejoice in hope of the glory of God. (Romans 4:24-5:2)

Now when Yeshua had come into Peter's house, He saw his wife's mother lying sick with a fever. So He touched her hand, and the fever left her. And she arose and served them. When evening had come, they brought to Him many who were demon-possessed. And He cast out the spirits with a word, and healed all who were sick, that it might be fulfilled which was spoken by Isaiah the prophet, saying: "He Himself took our infirmities and bore our sicknesses." (Matthew 8:14-17)

∽ THE PROPHETIC DESCRIPTION

The Servant died a substitutionary death for our sins:

But he was wounded because of our transgressions,
he was crushed because of our iniquities:
the chastisement of our welfare was upon him,
and with his stripes we were healed.
All we like sheep did go astray,
we turned every one to his own way;
and the LORD has made to light on him
the iniquity of us all. (Isaiah 53:5-6)

This is the very heart of the prophecy! The death of the Servant would be redemptive; it was God's way of securing atonement for you and me.

Peter recognized that the death of Yeshua was a
substitutionary sacrifice for the sins of humankind. This is
reflected in his early speeches in the Book of Acts:

> *The God of Abraham, Isaac, and Jacob, the God of our
> fathers, glorified His Servant Yeshua, whom you delivered
> up and denied in the presence of Pilate, when he was
> determined to let Him go. But you denied the Holy One
> and the Just, and asked for a murderer to be granted to you,
> and killed the Prince of life, whom God raised from the
> dead, of which we are witnesses.*

> *And His name, through faith in His name, has made this
> man strong, whom you see and know. Yes, the faith which
> comes through Him has given him this perfect soundness in
> the presence of you all. "Yet now, brethren, I know that you
> did it in ignorance, as did also your rulers. But those things
> which God foretold by the mouth of all His prophets, that the
> Messiah would suffer, He has thus fulfilled. (Acts 3:13-18)*

Luke further confirmed this, in his account of the meeting
between the Apostle Philip and an Ethiopian eunuch:

> *So Philip ran to him, and heard him reading the prophet
> Isaiah, and said, "Do you understand what you are
> reading?" And he said, "How can I, unless someone guides
> me?" And he asked Philip to come up and sit with him.
> The place in the Scripture, which he read, was this: "He
> was led as a sheep to the slaughter; And as a lamb before
> its shearer is silent, So He opened not His mouth. In His
> humiliation His justice was taken away, And who will
> declare His generation? For His life is taken from the
> earth." So the eunuch answered Philip and said, "I ask you,*

*of whom does the prophet say this, of himself or of some
other man?" Then Philip opened his mouth, and beginning
at this Scripture, preached Yeshua to him. (Acts 8:30-35)*

∞ THE PROPHETIC DESCRIPTION

The Servant suffered a humiliating death:

> *By oppression and judgment he was taken away,
> and with his generation who did reason?
> for he was cut off out of the land of the living,
> for the transgression of my people to whom the stroke was due.
> And they made his grave with the wicked,
> and with the rich his tomb;
> although he had done no violence,
> neither was any deceit in his mouth. (Isaiah 53:8-9)*

The death destined for the Servant was not only to be
sacrificial and redemptive, but also humiliating. This is
consistent with the rest of the prophecy, which describes
in detail the rejection of the Servant by the people He
had come to serve.

∞ THE NEW TESTAMENT FULFILLMENT

The account in the Book of Mark detailed the depths of
degradation and humiliation heaped upon Yeshua:

> *And when they crucified Him, they divided His garments,
> casting lots for them to determine what every man should
> take. Now it was the third hour, and they crucified Him.
> And the inscription of His accusation was written above:
> THE KING OF THE JEWS. With Him they also
> crucified two robbers, one on His right and the other on
> His left. So the Scripture was fulfilled which says, "And*

*He was numbered with the transgressors." And those who
passed by blasphemed Him, wagging their heads and
saying, "Aha! You who destroy the temple and build it in
three days, save Yourself, and come down from the cross!"
Likewise the chief priests also, mocking among themselves
with the scribes, said, "He saved others; Himself He
cannot save. Let the Messiah, the King of Israel, descend
now from the cross, that we may see and believe." Even
those who were crucified with Him reviled Him.*

*Now when the sixth hour had come, there was darkness
over the whole land until the ninth hour. And at the ninth
hour Yeshua cried out with a loud voice, saying, "Eloi, Eloi,
lama sabachthani?" which is translated, "My God, My
God, why have You forsaken Me?" Some of those who
stood by, when they heard that, said, "Look, He is calling
for Elijah!" Then someone ran and filled a sponge full of
sour wine, put it on a reed, and offered it to Him to drink,
saying, "Let Him alone; let us see if Elijah will come to
take Him down." (Mark 15:24-36)*

∞ THE PROPHETIC DESCRIPTION

The Servant's sacrifice is viewed in Isaiah as an offering for sin:

*Yet it pleased the LORD to crush him by disease;
to see if his soul would offer itself in restitution,
that he might see his seed, prolong his days,
and that the purpose of the LORD might prosper by his
hand. (Isaiah 53:10)*

The death of the Servant is compared to the sacrifice
in the Temple known as the *asham*. This word is
translated as "trespass offering," "guilt offering" or
simply "offering." The death of the Servant in Isaiah

53 is clearly viewed by the prophet as a trespass offering—the offering designed both for the removal of guilt and its implied restitution.

∞ THE NEW TESTAMENT FULFILLMENT

The Letter to the Hebrews, the author of which is unknown, is one of the most important parts of the New Testament for Jewish people to read and understand. It presumes a certain degree of familiarity with the Hebrew Scriptures, as the writer demonstrates that Yeshua fulfills the Messianic expectations of the earlier Jewish writings, including Isaiah 53:

> *But Messiah came as High Priest of the good things to come, with the greater and more perfect tabernacle not made with hands, that is, not of this creation. Not with the blood of goats and calves, but with His own blood He entered the Most Holy Place once for all, having obtained eternal redemption. For if the blood of bulls and goats and the ashes of a heifer, sprinkling the unclean, sanctifies for the purifying of the flesh, how much more shall the blood of Messiah, who through the eternal Spirit offered Himself without spot to God, cleanse your conscience from dead works to serve the living God? (Hebrews 9:1-14)*

∞ THE PROPHETIC DESCRIPTION

The Servant justifies many:

> *Of the travail of his soul he shall see to the full,*
> *even My servant, who by his knowledge*
> *did justify the Righteous One to the many,*
> *and their iniquities he did bear. (Isaiah 53:11)*

The death of the Servant was designed to accomplish something very specific: our atonement! According to the prophet, he would bear our iniquities—the Hebrew word for "iniquities" means "crooked" or "bent" as compared to the straight line of the Torah. The Hebrew word "justified" is drawn from the term that means "righteous." In other words, because the Servant died for our sins, we can be viewed as righteous by God. Not that we actually become righteous, although the trajectory of our lives once we are forgiven of our sin would be to move towards greater righteousness; of course, this is a lifetime process. Through the Servant and his atoning death, we can be forgiven and transformed.

∞ THE NEW TESTAMENT FULFILLMENT

The author of the Book of Hebrews described the way in which the sacrifice of Yeshua fulfills the demands of the Torah, especially the requirements of the sacrificial system. His bearing our iniquities does what the sacrifice of animals in the Temple could never truly accomplish; the Temple offerings were only shadows of the reality to come in Yeshua.

> *And every priest stands ministering daily and offering repeatedly the same sacrifices, which can never take away sins. But this Man, after He had offered one sacrifice for sins forever, sat down at the right hand of God, from that time waiting till His enemies are made His footstool. For by one offering He has perfected forever those who are being sanctified. But the Holy Spirit also witnesses to us; for after He had said before, "This is the covenant that I will make with them after those days, says the Lord: I will put My laws into their hearts, and in their minds I will write them," then He adds, "Their sins and their lawless deeds I will remember no more."*

Now where there is remission of these, there is no longer an offering for sin. Therefore, brethren, having boldness to enter the Holiest by the blood of Yeshua, by a new and living way which He consecrated for us, through the veil, that is, His flesh... (Hebrews 10:11-20)

☞ THE PROPHETIC DESCRIPTION

The Servant died and rose from the grave:

> *... that he might see his seed, prolong his days,*
> *and that the purpose of the LORD might prosper by his*
> *hand. (Isaiah 53:10)*

> *Therefore will I divide him a portion among the great,*
> *and he shall divide the spoil with the mighty;*
> *because he bared his soul unto death,*
> *and was numbered with the transgressors;*
> *yet he bore the sin of many,*
> *and made intercession for the transgressors. (Isaiah 53:12)*

The predictions found in the latter verses of Isaiah chapter 53 indicate that the Servant would die—and yet would somehow "prolong his days" and receive a reward from the Lord. This implies a resurrection.

☞ THE NEW TESTAMENT FULFILLMENT

He died:

> *After this, Yeshua, knowing that all things were now accomplished, that the Scripture might be fulfilled, said, "I thirst!" Now a vessel full of sour wine was sitting there; and they filled a sponge with sour wine, put it on hyssop, and put it to His mouth. So when Yeshua had received the sour*

wine, He said, "It is finished!" And bowing His head, He gave up His spirit. (John 19:28-30)

And Yeshua cried out with a loud voice, and breathed His last. Then the veil of the temple was torn in two from top to bottom. So when the centurion, who stood opposite Him, saw that He cried out like this and breathed His last, he said, "Truly this Man was the Son of God!" (Mark 15:37-39)

He rose from the dead:

Now after the Sabbath, as the first day of the week began to dawn, Mary Magdalene and the other Mary came to see the tomb. And behold, there was a great earthquake; for an angel of the Lord descended from heaven, and came and rolled back the stone from the door, and sat on it.

His countenance was like lightning, and his clothing as white as snow. And the guards shook for fear of him, and became like dead men. But the angel answered and said to the women, "Do not be afraid, for I know that you seek Yeshua who was crucified. "He is not here; for He is risen, as He said. Come, see the place where the Lord lay. "And go quickly and tell His disciples that He is risen from the dead, and indeed He is going before you into Galilee; there you will see Him. Behold, I have told you." So they went out quickly from the tomb with fear and great joy, and ran to bring His disciples word. And as they went to tell His disciples, behold, Yeshua met them, saying, "Rejoice!" So they came and held Him by the feet and worshiped Him. (Matthew 28:1-9)

In his letter to the Roman believers in Yeshua, Paul wrote,

Paul, a bondservant of Yeshua the Messiah, called to be an Apostle, separated to the Gospel of God which He promised

before through His prophets in the Holy Scriptures,
concerning His Son Yeshua Messiah our Lord, who was
born of the seed of David according to the flesh, and declared
to be the Son of God with power according to the Spirit of
holiness, by the resurrection from the dead. (Romans 1:1-4)

CONCLUSION

One could argue that it is impossible to figure out who
fulfills the prophecy in Isaiah 53. There has been a long
list of suggested candidates from both within and without
the Jewish community. Everyone from Jeremiah to Rabbi
Akiba has been suggested; recently I heard an Orthodox
rabbi claim that Martin Luther King was a fulfillment of
Isaiah 53! However, we should take our comparison of
the Old and New Testament texts very seriously. Only
one person has really fulfilled Isaiah chapter 53 to the
degree described above.

It is only fair to acknowledge the objections that some in
the Jewish community have to the possibility that Yeshua
is the Messiah, and we will address some of these in the
next chapter. However, as you continue reading, I believe
you will be surprised by how Judaism over the centuries
has believed in the coming of a suffering Messiah. So
keep reading—and keep thinking!

CHAPTER 10:
JEWISH OBJECTIONS EXPLAINED

Jewish spiritual leaders have been responding to the question of whether or not Isaiah chapter 53 refers to Jesus for centuries. After all, it is clear from even a quick reading of the New Testament that the early Jewish disciples quoted quite often from this passage. From the encounter between Phillip and the Ethiopian eunuch to the sermons of Peter, there is no doubt that the early Messianic Jews found Isaiah 53 to be foundational to their faith.

As mentioned in the beginning of the book, these days it is commonly thought within the Jewish community that when someone who was born Jewish accepts Jesus as their Messiah, they have somehow converted to "Christianity." We would contest this idea, and although a few aspects of it are true, the heart of the matter—whether or not Jesus is the Jewish Messiah—should be evaluated on its own merits. If Isaiah chapter 53 is indeed fulfilled by Yeshua, then clearly He should be embraced as the Messiah.

The problem we face and the tension we sense stems from the perceived alienation between "Christianity" and the Jewish community. The chasm is both theological and sociological, and the objectivity of the discussion is often quickly lost. Sadly, the Jewish people have been persecuted in the name of Jesus, which makes the issue a volatile one.

When it comes right down to it, perhaps this is the major objection to the idea of Isaiah 53 being fulfilled in Yeshua. It is not that there is so much doubt about the words of the text or even the credibility of the New Testament. But because the gap seems so wide and the alienation so severe, it is simply hard to imagine that a person could be Jewish and believe in Jesus.

Yet today, there are tens of thousands of Jewish people who believe in Yeshua—often called Messianic Jews— living in the United States or Israel and in almost every nation where there is a Jewish community. Often, these Jewish people who believe in Yeshua maintain Jewish traditions, celebrate the Jewish holidays and strongly identify with the Jewish community and with the modern State of Israel. The main difference between Messianic Jews and the more mainstream Jewish community is that Messianic Jews believe that Yeshua is the Messiah.

Over the centuries, the Jewish leadership has developed a number of objections to the possibility that Yeshua is the fulfillment of Isaiah chapter 53. It is not our intention to go into great depth, as many of the arguments are quite technical, theological and even depend upon how one might interpret the Hebrew phrasing.

There is a wonderful statement by a Gentile Christian who loved the Jewish people: "When the plain sense of Scripture makes common sense, seek no other sense." This "golden rule of interpretation" was penned by David L. Cooper, a Hebrew scholar who authored many books on the subject of Messianic prophecy, and wrote quite extensively on Isaiah chapter 53.

Let's look briefly at some of the objections to Yeshua being the Jewish Messiah, and then at the Messianic Jewish view.

ONE MESSIAH OR TWO?

Traditionally, mainstream Judaism has taught that there is only one Messiah—although there is a minority line of thought that speaks of two Messiahs: one to die in the final war of Gog and Magog, and the other to reign on the throne of David. But the dominant tradition is that Messiah, the son of David, will come in the end of days and will accomplish a number of tasks:

∞ He will raise the dead

∞ He will be victorious over the enemies of Israel

∞ He will reign as king in Israel with Jerusalem as His capital

∞ He will put an end to war, and peace will fill the earth

The Jewish community thus believes that Yeshua could not be the Messiah because He did not accomplish these tasks.

THE RESPONSE

Two pictures of the Messiah are found in the Hebrew Scriptures. One is that of a victorious Messiah reigning in righteousness. The other is a picture of a humble Messiah who would die as a substitute for the sins of humanity. The idea of a suffering Messiah is not outside the realm of Jewish tradition. Many Jewish thinkers and writers, both past and present, have held to this view.

While it is commonly taught that the Messiah's role is to restore the Kingdom of God, there is also a basis for a suffering Messiah in Jewish thought. The basis for believing that Messiah would come humbly and suffer for the sins of the Jewish people is found in our chapter, Isaiah 53. Let's look at the sources:

But he was wounded because of our transgressions, he was crushed because of our iniquities: the chastisement of our welfare was upon him, and with his stripes we were healed. (Isaiah 53:5)

Messiah Son of David who loves Jerusalem… Elijah takes him by the head… and says "You must bear the sufferings and wounds by which the Almighty chastises you for Israel's sins" and so it is written, He was wounded for our transgressions, bruised for our iniquities. (Midrash Konen; 11th century)

The children of the world are members one of another. When the Holy One desires to give healing to the world, he smites one just man amongst them, and for his sake heals all the rest. From where do we learn this? From the saying [Isaiah 53:5], "He was wounded for our transgressions, bruised for our iniquities. (Zohar, Numbers, Pinchus 218a)

Yet it pleased the LORD to crush him by disease; to see if his soul would offer itself in restitution, that he might see his seed, prolong his days, and that the purpose of the LORD might prosper by his hand (Isaiah 53:10)

The Messiah, in order to atone for them both [Adam and David], will make his soul a trespass offering [Isaiah 53:10] as it is written next to this parashah "Behold my servant" [Isaiah 52:13]. (Midrash Aseret Memrot)

There are other passages that speak about the Messiah dying for our sins, such as Zechariah 12:10:

> *And I will pour upon the house of David, and upon the inhabitants of Jerusalem, the spirit of grace and of supplication; and they shall look to Me because they have thrust him through; and they shall mourn for him, as one mourns for his only son, and shall be in bitterness for him, as one that is in bitterness for his first-born.*

The choices regarding the coming of the Messiah are simple. We could believe in one Messiah who will come as king—this is the traditional Jewish view, yet it ignores the prophecies of a suffering Messiah. We could believe in two Messiahs, one to die and the other to reign as king (Messiah the son of Joseph and Messiah the son of David)—a minority opinion within traditional Judaism.

The third view is that held by Messianic Jews and believing Christians—that there is one Messiah, but that the prophecies in the Hebrew Scriptures point to two distinct roles: dying for sin and reigning as king in the Messianic era. We believe that Yeshua the Messiah came the first time to die for our sins as a humble Servant (and rose from the dead, as predicted by Isaiah and confirmed by the Gospel writers), and that He will return a second time to reign as king.

CONTEMPORARY OBJECTIONS

The contemporary objections to Isaiah 53 are varied. They include a disdain for the concept of animal sacrifice and difficulty in understanding why God would require the death of His Son to forgive sin. It is not hard to see that Isaiah 53 challenges the mindset of most contemporary Jews and Gentiles.

At an even deeper level, the very idea that God is holy and that humanity is predisposed to displease our Creator is contrary to the more optimistic view of ourselves that we prefer to cultivate. Furthermore, the assertion that God must judge sin and sinners because He is just, clashes with our modern notions of the "nice" God we wish to envision.

Also, many of us living in the 21st century have an anti-supernatural bias. We quickly dismiss whatever is deemed "non-rational," supernatural or old-fashioned and archaic—which is the way many of us view the teachings of the Bible.

THE RESPONSE

We have been raised with a rationalistic mindset, but we have never had the opportunity to assess objectively whether or not rationalism is right. Although raised in the humanistic belief in the goodness of humankind, many of us have serious doubts about this notion. We sense that there is something wrong in our viewpoint, but we are not quite sure what it is or how to solve it.

Maybe it is time for us to put some of our prejudices aside and open our hearts and minds to the possibility that there is a personal God who has spoken to us, and that He has something important for us to understand. Maybe we need to take a step back from the way we were raised and reconsider whether anti-supernaturalism is correct, justifiable and the only way to view life. Let's take a fresh look at spirituality and faith, which have been the source of considerable beauty, nobility of soul and humanitarianism.

Is the Nation of Israel the Fulfillment of Isaiah Chapter 53?

Judaism teaches that Isaiah 53 is fulfilled in the suffering and survival of the nation of Israel, which bore the sins of the Gentile nations. Rashi and other sages developed this response during the Middle Ages, when Jewish people were often persecuted for not believing in Jesus. This persecution is a blight on history and does not reflect the truth as God intended it to be lived out. It is understandable that some of our great rabbis chose to interpret Isaiah 53 in this way.

The Response

Although we understand the reasons, this explanation does not reflect the clear teaching found in the text of Isaiah 53. Here are a few reasons why this prophecy cannot refer to the nation of Israel, but rather, must be fulfilled in the Messiah:

1. Israel is not an innocent sufferer, as is the individual described in the passage.

Israel as a nation was sinful, as described in the preceding chapters of the Book of Isaiah – especially chapters 1 and 5.

2. Israel is not a silent sufferer, as is the individual described in the passage.

Many excellent arguments have been made to demonstrate that the Jewish people have never been silent sufferers. Even when the Holocaust is used as an illustration of Israel's suffering without complaint, it can be equally demonstrated that our people had well-organized resistance movements and only suffered silently when they were unaware of the horror and reality of the Final Solution.

3. Israel never died, as did the individual
   described in the passage.

It is evident that Israel has never died; the nation has continued to maintain a distinct national existence throughout the centuries. Some might say that the nation of Israel died, in a sense, during the Holocaust and therefore the resurrection passage in Isaiah 53:10-12 is fulfilled in the rebirth of the modern State of Israel. But this is a difficult argument to sustain, as the passage would have to be interpreted allegorically or symbolically and the language does not warrant this method of interpretation.

4. The text points to the suffering of an individual,
   not a nation.

This is very clear from the words of the text. One has to really allegorize the words of Isaiah in order to make them apply to the entire nation. In addition, the theme of redemptive suffering in rabbinic tradition is specifically focused on traditions related to the suffering of an individual called Messiah son of Joseph.

5. The nation of Israel is the beneficiary
   of the Servant's sacrifice.

Perhaps the strongest argument against Isaiah 53 being a reference to the nation of Israel is found in verse eight. In this verse, the prophet described the one who would suffer as being "cut off out of the land of the living, for the transgressions of my people to whom the stroke was due." The Hebrew term translated as "cut off" refers to the death of the individual and, if taken literally, clearly refers to an individual person dying for the sins of God's people, the Jewish people.

Therefore, it is fair to ask the question, "How can Israel be killed on behalf of Israel?" This is impossible. The subject of Isaiah 53 simply cannot be Israel as a nation.

Many other arguments can be made to demonstrate that the traditional Jewish interpretation of Isaiah 53 as a reference to the nation of Israel is simply not an accurate interpretation. Rather, it is an explanation driven by history, culture and politics—but not by the text.

CHAPTER 11:
ISAIAH 53 AND YOU

THE IMPLICATIONS AND BENEFITS
OF THE SERVANT'S DEATH

Within three decades after the death of Yeshua, Paul, the rabbi from Tarsus, wrote these words as a commentary on Isaiah 53:

> *He made him who knew no sin to become sin on our behalf that we might become the righteousness of God in him. (2 Corinthians 5:21)*

The rabbi understood the chapter's teaching that the Servant, though innocent, died for our sins. Understandably, the spiritual dimensions to the sacrifice of the Servant are still challenging for us to grasp, as most of us have been raised to be skeptical of anything we cannot see or prove in a laboratory!

This is where faith comes into the picture—not only faith in God, but openness to the possibility that the Bible is trustworthy, including what it says about the meaning of this one man's death. Trust and faith are twin sisters, and a willingness to trust the Bible and its Author is not easy for us. Yet sometimes even a small glimmer of faith will enable a person to get past the everyday to the spiritual. You would be amazed at how real, logical and tangible spiritual truths can become when comprehended by faith.

I cannot explain exactly why the death of the Servant can impact your life today, but from my own experience and that of many others, I know it is possible. You will only be able to grasp this yourself if you open your heart to God and invite Him to reveal to you what the death and resurrection of the Servant can mean to you. It is something profoundly personal that goes beyond common logic and touches the deepest part of the soul.

Some things are best proven by personal experience. From the love of a spouse or a child to the beauty of a sunset, it is impossible to measure the things that give us the greatest joys in life; they simply must be felt. The impact of the death of the Servant on your life today, if understood with faith, can be the most rewarding thing you experience.

Isaiah makes it clear that Messiah's sacrifice and the punishment He suffered was rightly ours: "But he was wounded because of our transgressions, he was crushed because of our iniquities…" Although He was blameless in God's eyes, He voluntarily suffered for our wrongs, for the sake of our healing and the restoration of our relationship with God: "…the chastisement of our welfare was upon him, and with his stripes we were healed."

The good news is that His death and resurrection satisfied God's justice. When we recognize that Isaiah 53 points to Yeshua the Messiah and we turn from our sins, then we can have peace with God and know the joy of forgiveness that God offers through the death of Yeshua.

How should we respond to God's love showered upon us in the Messiah?

I am sure you still have lots of questions, and I remember the moment when I was ready to accept Yeshua as the Messiah. I still had questions, but somehow deep inside I knew that it was true. I did not have it all figured out as to how I could be Jewish and believe in Jesus, but I knew enough at that point to recognize that because Jesus was Jewish, He would help me figure it all out—and He did!

What He did for me and for so many other Messianic Jews, He can certainly do for you. Of course, you can also believe in Yeshua if you are not Jewish!

Wouldn't now be a good time for you to receive the Messiah?

You might pray the following prayer:

> *Dear God of Abraham, Isaac and Jacob, I know I am one of the sheep that has gone astray and turned to my own way. But, Lord, I also recognize that You laid the penalty of my sins on Yeshua the Messiah. I believe this and want to accept Him as my Lord. Thank You for sending Yeshua to die in my place allowing me to begin a personal relationship with You. Thank You for providing my atonement through Yeshua.*

You might also meditate on these passages of Scripture found in the New Testament:

> *…if you confess with your mouth the Lord Yeshua and believe in your heart that God has raised Him from the dead, you will be saved. For with the heart one believes unto righteousness, and with the mouth confession is made unto salvation. (Romans 10:9-10)*

> *But as many as received Him, to them He gave the right to become children of God, to those who believe in His name. (John 1:12)*

If you prayed this simple prayer, you can be assured that God has forgiven you of your sin and that you have received the gift of eternal life—a life that begins now and lasts forever.

May we help you grow in your faith? Please consider enrolling in our four-week online and "snail mail" Bible study series. It is free, and I am sure you will benefit from it.

Please accept our invitation for ongoing Bible study and go to:

www.Isaiah53.com

You can also write to
241 East 51st Street
New York, NY 10022

or call 1-888-2-YESHUA.

We would also be happy to receive
your questions by email at info@isaiah53.com

CHAPTER 12:
YOU ARE NOT ALONE

It helps to know that there are other Jewish people who believe Yeshua is the fulfillment of Isaiah 53. We can be strengthened and filled with greater courage when we know we are not alone. The following are stories of Jewish people who have found the prophecy of Isaiah to be true—and fulfilled in Yeshua!

ALAN SHORE

As I entered young adulthood, I was like every other Jewish person I had ever known—hearing the name Jesus produced in me a complex set of emotions, dominated mainly by embarrassment.

I was baffled by the plethora of churches, crosses, statues, paintings and street preachers that I saw in virtually every direction I turned. I couldn't fathom it. Add to this the suspicion of the Christian world that was practically encoded in my DNA, and you won't be surprised that getting to know Jesus was not high on my list of priorities.

Besides, what could His death possibly have to do with me? He had been crucified. So what? It was a sad but distant tragedy. What could the death of a man twenty centuries ago possibly mean to me today?

It was during this time of questioning that someone showed me Isaiah 53. These verses leapt out at me. For the first time, I was able to make a connection with this helpless sufferer who had been given an oversized portion of the rejection, grief, humiliation and suffering that seemed to characterize the history of my people. Taken together with other pieces of knowledge that were coming my way, I could see that it was Jesus.

Isaiah 53 helped me to understand two things of critical importance. The first is that the suffering of the Man of Sorrows is meaningful—not only in the abstract, but also in concrete ways that help us to understand ourselves and our circumstances. As the suffering of Yeshua becomes real to us, it somehow helps us to bear our own suffering. After I made this connection, I could no longer see Jesus as alien to Jewish life. It was quite the opposite. He seemed to me to be the embodiment of Jewish experience for all time—destined to suffer at the hands of the world, yet finally to be vindicated by God.

ISRAEL COHEN

Once I was in the Navy and away from my parents, I had the opportunity to do some new things—not all of them strictly kosher. One afternoon as I sat alone in the barracks, a young sailor came over to me and asked if I was Jewish. When I told him I was, he asked me to teach him about being Jewish (obviously he was not!). As I started to tell him, he interrupted me: "Can you teach me about being Jewish from the Bible?" I got hold of a Jewish Bible, but didn't know where to turn. So he asked me to turn to Isaiah, to the 53rd chapter.

"Read this aloud," he said, and I did. At first I thought I had the wrong Bible. Was this sailor tricking me? It sounded so much like what my Christian friends used to say about Jesus!

My friend explained that Jesus was Jewish, the New Testament was written by Jews and that it tells all about the Jewish Messiah. Never in my life had I been so confused!

But after three hours of talking and reading from both of our Bibles, especially Isaiah 53 in my Jewish Bible, my confusion started to disappear. I understood that I needed the forgiveness offered by Jesus, the Jewish Messiah. But I also knew I was Jewish and that Jews do not believe in Jesus!

I was so torn that I actually cried that sleepless night, pulling my blanket over my head so the others could not hear my weeping. I could no longer resist doing what I knew I had to do: I prayed to God and told Him that I believed Jesus was really the Jewish Messiah.

I asked His forgiveness for the many ways I had failed to live as I knew God wanted me to live. A few moments later, I went peacefully to sleep—and woke up to a brand new life.

PAULA MICHELSON

As a 14-year-old big sister, I remember well when my brother, Ron, was studying for his Bar Mitzvah. While he was supposed to be paying attention in Hebrew class to his *Haftarah*, I guess he got bored and started restlessly looking at other writings in his Bible.

He was a little surprised to discover a book, Isaiah, that he had never heard of and a chapter that grabbed his attention the instant he read it. When he came home, he found that our parents were out and he cautiously asked me into his bedroom. He gave me his Bible and had me sit down while he closed the door. This was a very unusual act, since our parents' rule was that none of our doors were to be closed during the day unless someone was ill. I looked down at the chapter to which he had opened his Bible and began to read.

I remember reading these words as if it were yesterday: "Who would have believed our report? And to whom has the arm of the Lord been revealed?" (Isaiah 53:1) After I read the entire chapter, my brother asked me, almost afraid of what I would answer, "Who do you think Isaiah was speaking about?"

At that moment, I knew. But it was a big risk to say what I did: "I think it's Jesus."

To my surprise, he agreed. "But what," he asked, "do we do about this?"

We agreed to keep it our secret for the time being, frightened that our parents would throw us out of the house!

Years later, my brother and I became convinced that Jesus, Yeshua, was the Messiah. I wish I had known as a teenager what I know now: knowing our Messiah does not cause us to abandon our Jewish identity. Instead, it allows us to become what God always intended—faithful Jews united with Messiah.

Dr. Dan Goldberg

Many years ago, our family lived in Los Angeles, on a block that was mostly Gentile—so we were noticed by our neighbors. One day when I returned home from high school, I was informed of a curious request. A Gentile lady had asked permission for me to come visit her. I had no idea what it was all about, and when I went to her home, she said, "Sit down, I want to read you something." It was Isaiah 53. It was the first section of the Bible I had ever heard.

After my brother Louis, who was eight years older, came to faith in the Messiah, he told my parents that he had become a believer. They were very upset, as they had come from Poland and were familiar with the persecution of the Jewish people there. But Louis' faith impressed me. Another Gentile woman in the neighborhood gave me a Gideon Bible, and after reading the Gospel of John, I followed in my brother's footsteps and became a believer in Jesus in 1948 at the age of eighteen.

I don't even remember the name of the woman who first showed me Isaiah 53. I only remember that somehow, God impressed in my mind that this passage, written by a Jewish prophet, was talking about Jesus. That impression stayed with me. I knew very little about Jesus at the time—only that He was said to have died for our sins, and this seemed to coincide with the Bible passage that was read to me on that day. As I learned more about the Bible, Isaiah 53 became even more meaningful to me—and I still have the Gideon Bible that woman gave me all those years ago.

JEFF KRAN

At the time when my spiritual search began to intensify, I was pursuing a serious interest in my Jewish faith and had some deep questions. Although my parents were more or less secular, I had been deeply influenced by my grandfather, who lived with us for a time and who took me to synagogue with him. Although I was living what I thought was a pretty upstanding life, I was troubled by the supposed need of atonement through blood sacrifices expressed in Leviticus 17. This led me to look more closely at Isaiah 53, and I had questions. To whom did this refer? Did this passage relate to Messiah? Was it a possible solution to my dilemma?

I spent much time trying to discern who the passage was about. I remember looking at our family Jewish Bible and the commentary it contained. It spoke of Israel as the subject of Isaiah 53—but I couldn't square that interpretation with what I read. The passage referred to a person, not a nation. I remember thinking, "This looks like someone is doing the suffering for us, not Israel suffering for itself." That began to lead me towards believing that the Messiah is God's provision for our forgiveness. This put the concepts of atonement and Messiah together in my mind, which, in turn, led me to investigate the New Testament.

The big question was this: did Isaiah 53 refer to Jesus? As I started reading Matthew, the first book in the New Testament, I began checking the prophecies he referred to in the Hebrew Scriptures. As I did this, I started seeing how Yeshua fit the prophetic description of the sacrifice God had provided for my forgiveness. I saw how important this was because of the basic need for atonement that I had first seen in Leviticus 17. Isaiah 53 provided the key that unlocked my understanding of what God sent Yeshua to do for us.

LAWRENCE HIRSCH

My older brother, Alan, was always a seeker after truth. He really upset the family, to say the least, when he came home from the army one weekend with a Bible and some religious literature in his bags. I was about fourteen years old, and I still remember all the shouting and the tears as my mom and dad confronted him.

On one occasion, Alan opened the Bible and asked if he could read a passage of Scripture to me. I agreed to listen. He didn't tell me which passage, but he began to read from Isaiah 53. When he finished, I said, "Well, that was all about Jesus, wasn't it? That is in the New Testament, isn't it?"

Of course, you could have blown me over with a feather when my brother revealed that he had just read from the Jewish prophet Isaiah. He also informed me that Isaiah had written these words 700 years before Jesus lived—yet it seemed so obvious to me that Isaiah was speaking about Jesus!

I didn't let on how much this had impacted me; I kept it all to myself. I was especially taken aback by the words in verse three: "He was despised, and forsaken of men, a man of pains, and acquainted with disease…" Had we, as the Jewish people, rejected our very own Messiah? How could this be?

It took me several months to fully grasp the significance of these verses and the implications for my life. I knew that believing in Jesus would mean going against all that I had been brought up to believe as a Jew, and I would face much anger and opposition from my family and my people. Yet I could not deny the truth of what I read in Isaiah 53, and I too came to accept Yeshua as my Messiah.

A PERSONAL POSTSCRIPT

I was raised in a traditional Jewish home. We were part of a Young Israel synagogue, which is a modern Orthodox Jewish movement based in the United States. My family was not especially religious and I did not go to *Yeshiva,* but everything I learned about the Jewish religion was from the Young Israel synagogue and Hebrew school I attended in Queens, New York. I went to *Talmud Torah cheder* (class) five days a week between the ages of eight and thirteen. Many of my friends did attend the more religious *Yeshiva,* and I also felt comfortable in their world. Even though I was a rebellious young man, I had the highest regard for my Hebrew-school teachers and my rabbi…though I will admit to being the one who sent some of those spitballs flying in the middle of reading long sections of Hebrew prayers!

My own journey was not unlike that of many of my peers. I dropped out of college and went to California with my hippie friends, looking for the meaning of life and some fun! It was during that time that my two closest friends, who were Jewish, became believers in Jesus. They shared the message with me, and part of their "proof" that Jesus was the Messiah was based upon their understanding of Isaiah 53.

When I read the chapter for myself, I was struck by its simplicity and power and wondered why I had never before seen this passage during my years of Jewish education and study of the *Tanakh.* After a time of serious reflection and reading the New Testament, I became a believer in Yeshua. I saw that Yeshua fulfilled the prophecy penned by Isaiah more than 700 years earlier with undeniable accuracy.

After this life-changing decision in November of 1970, I returned home from California in the late spring of 1971 to attend college. I did not tell my parents that I had become a Messianic Jew, and I did not tell them that I was going to attend a Bible college. I was scared to death of what they would think and how they would react!

I remember the day that I hitchhiked home in my faded blue overalls. I knew it would be important to share what I had found with my parents. I entered my home and was relieved to find that my parents were very glad to see me. We ate, we talked and then finally my mother asked the dreaded question, "How long will you be staying?"

I responded, "I am back for good."

"Will you be going back to college?" she asked. As a university dropout, I was a Jewish mother's worst nightmare...almost!

"I am planning on going back to college," I replied, and then sort of coughed as I said that it would be a Bible college.

My mother looked at me and asked, "What's a Bible college?"

"That's where they study the Bible," I responded.

My mother looked at me quizzically and said, "Why are you going to study the Bible?" I told both of my parents that it was a wonderful book and that everyone should try reading it. After all, I had been a good student at Hebrew school!

My mother and father paused and looked at one another, at which point I realized that I could not continue avoiding the subject that was foremost in my mind. I told them of my decision to become a follower of Jesus.

My father gasped and my mother burst into tears, and they began arguing with each other. My mother accused my father of not raising me "religious enough," and my father accused my mother of raising me overly religious. They also expressed anger at my grandparents for being so old-fashioned and Orthodox.

At that point, my parents asked me to leave the house. They began laying down the law regarding with whom I could speak and with whom I could not speak about Jesus, as well as what I could and could not do regarding my beliefs. They said that I could not speak to my grandparents, neighbors, or my sisters. Of course, I told them that this was not acceptable. My mother then forbade me from bringing crosses into the house, going to church or reading the New Testament. Back and forth it went.

That evening—which was supposed to be my last night at home, I asked my mom if I could show her why I believed Jesus was the Messiah. She said yes, as long as I did not use the New Testament. I sat down and began reading Isaiah 53 to her from an English translation of the Bible. As I read, I fully expected that my mother would see that Isaiah 53 referred to Jesus and she would realize He was the Messiah. I thought she would also understand how deeply connected this decision was with our Jewish heritage, and she would be reassured that in no way had I rejected this precious inheritance. That would resolve the conflict—or so I thought!

Instead, my mother had fallen asleep by verse eight. I woke her up and asked if I could keep reading. She nodded in a sleepy stupor. When I finished the passage, I asked her, "So what do you think?"

She said, "I told you not to read the New Testament to me!"

"But Mom," I responded. "That's our Bible. Isaiah is a Jewish prophet."

"I don't care," she answered. "Don't ever bring this up to me again!"

My beloved mother (may the Lord give rest to her soul) was typical of many Jewish people. Isaiah chapter 53, in my estimation, is one of the clearest prophecies of the person and work of Messiah in the entirety of the Hebrew Scriptures. I realize that not everyone who reads Isaiah 53 understands the Messianic fulfillment of this passage. But I am hoping that you will have an open mind and that you will draw your own conclusions.

Appendix: Additional Prophecies Pointing to Yeshua the Jewish Messiah

1. The origin and birthplace of the Messiah

∞ Prophecy: Micah 5:2 (5:1 in the Jewish Bible)

But you, Bethlehem Ephrathah, who are little to be among the thousands of Judah, out of you shall one come forth to Me that is to be ruler in Israel; whose goings forth are from of old, from ancient days.

∞ Fulfillment: Matthew 2:1

Now after Yeshua was born in Bethlehem of Judea in the days of Herod the king, behold, wise men from the East came to Jerusalem...

Bethlehem Ephrathah was in the territory of the tribe of Judah, five miles south of Jerusalem (see Ruth 1:2). There was another Bethlehem just northwest of Nazareth, but the birthplace of the Ruler was to be Bethlehem of Judah—and so it was (see Matthew 2:1 and Luke 2:4-7). It is clear that the Jews knew that the Messiah could not come from Nazareth, but that He would come from Bethlehem, the city of David (John 7:42).

The one born there was to be Ruler in Israel. When Pontius Pilate asked Yeshua if He was the King of the

Jews, He affirmed the title (Luke 23:3). But just claiming to be an earthly king alone would not qualify Yeshua as the Messiah, for the Messiah must be from everlasting (literally, from "days of eternity"). When Yeshua declared that "before Abraham was, I AM" (John 8:58), the Jewish people understood Him to be saying that He was from eternity. By His statement "I AM" (not "I was") He identified Himself with the God of Israel, who also called Himself "I AM" (Exodus 3:14).

2. THE BIRTH, MINISTRY AND VICTORY OF MESSIAH

∞ PROPHECY: GENESIS 3:15

And I will put enmity between you and the woman, and between your seed and her seed; they shall bruise your head, and you shall bruise their heel.

∞ FULFILLMENT:
GALATIANS 4:4; MATTHEW 27:62-63; 1 JOHN 3:8

But when the fullness of the time had come, God sent forth His Son, born of a woman. (Galatians 4:4)

On the next day, which followed the Day of Preparation, the chief priests and Pharisees gathered together to Pilate, saying, "Sir, we remember, while He was still alive, how [He] said, 'After three days I will rise.'" (Matthew 27:62-63)

For this purpose the Son of God was manifested, that He might destroy the works of the devil. (1 John 3:8).

The prophecy in Genesis 3:15 is the first Messianic prophecy in the Bible. It is spoken by God Himself to the serpent, Satan, who had successfully tempted Eve into disobeying God. In prophesying the ultimate demise of Satan, God said that the woman would bring forth a seed (a descendant) who would be at enmity with Satan. In addition to Galatians 4:4, the narratives concerning Yeshua's birth give ample evidence that He was born to Miriam (Mary), the wife of Joseph of Nazareth.

As to enmity with Satan, the most notable of the confrontations between Satan and Yeshua occurred in the wilderness at the beginning of Yeshua's ministry (Luke 4:1-12). Their enmity resulted in the death of the Messiah, but just as Genesis 3:15 predicted, Messiah's wounding was not a final wound, since He rose from the dead—as He Himself predicted (Matthew 27:63).

Finally, the prophecy of Genesis 3:15 is fulfilled in the ultimate destruction of Satan and his works by Messiah Yeshua. The Apostle John testifies that Yeshua came to destroy the works of Satan, to wield a death blow, as God said in Genesis. Revelation 20:10 depicts the final victory of Yeshua, the Seed of the woman, over the serpent.

3. THE MESSIAH IS A DESCENDANT OF ABRAHAM

∞ PROPHECY: GENESIS 12:1-3

Now the LORD said to Abram: "Get out of your country, and from your kindred, and from your father's house, to the land that I will show you. And I will make of you a great nation, and I will bless you, and make your name great; and you will be a blessing. 3 And I will bless them that bless you, and him that curses you will I curse; and in you shall all the families of the earth be blessed."

⌘ FULFILLMENT: MATTHEW 1:1

The Book of the genealogy of Yeshua the Messiah the son of Abraham.

It is obvious from the Old Testament that God chose Abraham to begin a heritage that would ultimately be a blessing, not only to Israel, but to the entire earth. Specifically, we know from Isaiah 42:1-8 that the way in which God would bless the Gentile nations of the earth was through His servant, the Messiah. Therefore, whoever claimed to be the Messiah of Israel must be one who was descended from Abraham, and whose ministry included not only the nation of Israel but the Gentiles as well.

Matthew clearly records in the genealogy of Yeshua that He is a descendant of Abraham. Yeshua obviously ministered to Jewish people during His earthly life, but also to Gentiles (for example, a Canaanite woman in Matthew 15:21-28, and a Roman soldier in Matthew 8:5-13). He sent out 72 of His followers to preach the Gospel, a number that many believe parallels the list of nations in Genesis 10. Finally, when Yeshua called Saul of Tarsus to be an apostle, His specific commission to Saul (or as he was known in the Roman world, Paul) was to "bear My name before Gentiles, kings, and the children of Israel" (Acts 9:5,15).

4. The Messiah is from the tribe of Judah

⌘ PROPHECY: GENESIS 49:10

The scepter shall not depart from Judah, nor a lawgiver from between his feet, until Shiloh comes; and to Him shall be the obedience of the people.

∞ FULFILLMENT: LUKE 3:33

...the son of Amminadab, the son of Ram, the son of Hezron, the son of Perez, the son of Judah.

From the first prophecy given to Abraham, the line of promise progressed through Isaac and then through Isaac's son, Jacob. On his deathbed, Jacob prophesied over his twelve sons, telling them what would happen to them in days to come (Genesis 49:1). Jacob predicted that the descendants of Judah would forever be the ones through whom kingship will pass. Therefore, the Messiah must be a descendant of Judah, which He was, as the New Testament verifies (Matthew 1:2-3; Luke 3:33).

Interestingly, the last king of Judah, Zedekiah, is told by God through the prophet Ezekiel to remove his crown that it might be restored to the One to Whom it rightfully belongs—obviously the anticipated Messiah (Ezekiel 21:25-27).

5. THE MESSIAH IS FROM THE HOUSE OF DAVID

∞ PROPHECY: 2 SAMUEL 7:12-13

When your days are fulfilled, and you shall sleep with your fathers, I will set up your seed after you, that shall proceed out of your body, and I will establish his kingdom. He shall build a house for My name, and I will establish the throne of his kingdom for ever.

∞ FULFILLMENT: LUKE 3:31

...the son of Melea, the son of Menna, the son of Mattathah, the son of Nathan, the son of David.

This prophecy, spoken to David, traces the Messianic line to one of his descendants. It refers in part to David's son, King Solomon, but there is a deeper Messianic meaning. Messiah would have to be a person from the tribe of Judah and from the House of David. This perpetual dynasty of the House of David—and Yeshua's fulfillment of the dynastic promises—is one of the best-attested Messianic relationships in all the Bible (see Psalm 89:30-38; Isaiah 9:1-7; Matthew 1:1; Luke 1:31-33, 69; Acts 2:30; 13:23; Romans 1:2-3; 2 Timothy 2:8; Revelation 3:7; 22:16).

6. MESSIAH WOULD BE BORN OF A VIRGIN

∞ PROPHECY: ISAIAH 7:14

Therefore the Lord Himself shall give you a sign: behold, the young woman [Hebrew "almah"] shall conceive, and bear a son, and shall call his name Immanuel.

∞ FULFILLMENT: MATTHEW 1:18, 22-23

Now the birth of Yeshua the Messiah was as follows: After His mother Mary was betrothed to Joseph, before they came together, she was found with child of the Holy Spirit. So all this was done that it might be fulfilled which was spoken by the Lord through the prophet, saying: "Behold, the virgin shall be with child, and bear a Son, and they shall call His name Immanuel," which is translated, "God with us."

This passage, which should be carefully studied in context, is a direct prophecy of the virgin birth of the Messiah (Luke 1:26-27). The translators of the Jewish Bible use the word "young woman" instead of "virgin"—but culturally, the Hebrew word *almah* almost always referred to an unmarried young woman, which in Isaiah's day implied virginity. In addition, the authors of the Septuagint, a Greek translation of the Old Testament completed before Yeshua's birth, translated this word as "virgin," which was its meaning in biblical Hebrew. Given the very explicit reference to this verse by Matthew (1:22-23), there can be no question that Miriam, the virgin mother of Yeshua, unquestionably fulfilled this prophecy about the birth of Messiah.

In the Bible, people's names describe their identities. The child's name, Immanuel, which means "God with us," indicates that this prophesied child would be God Himself walking among us.

7. THE MESSIAH IS GOD IN THE FLESH

⚭ PROPHECY: ISAIAH 9:6-7 (9:5-6 IN HEBREW)

For a child is born to us, a son is given to us; and the government is upon his shoulder; and his name is called Pele-joez-el-gibbor-Abi-ad-sar-shalom [translation: "Wonderful Counselor, Mighty God, Eternal Father, Prince of Peace"]; that the government may be increased, and of peace there be no end, upon the throne of David, and upon his kingdom, to establish it, and to uphold it through justice and through righteousness from henceforth even for ever. The zeal of the LORD of hosts will perform this.

⚭ FULFILLMENT: MATTHEW 1:1; JOHN 1:14

The Book of the genealogy of Yeshua the Messiah, the Son of David, the Son of Abraham. (Matthew 1:1)

And the Word became flesh and dwelt among us, and we beheld His glory, the glory as of the only begotten of the Father, full of grace and truth. (John 1:14)

These all-important names given to Messiah in Isaiah chapter 9 reveal His deity. Traditional Judaism does not teach that Messiah will be God, but this idea is clearly presented in the Hebrew Scriptures. The four names given to Messiah in Isaiah chapter 9 all point to the conclusion that this eternal ruler is God Himself. In fact, many Jewish versions of the Bible do not even translate the names, but rather transliterate them (change the Hebrew characters into English characters) so that their meaning is not obviously seen!

If these references to the Mighty God and Everlasting Father are not enough to demonstrate that Messiah is God, the Apostle John tells us that Yeshua is God who became flesh and dwelt among us. Having already established that Yeshua is the descendant of Abraham and David, it is easy to see that this one who is Wonderful, Counselor and the Prince of Peace is Yeshua, from Isaiah's words in Isaiah 11:1-5. There, the "stump of Jesse" (Jesse being David's father) is said to possess wisdom, understanding, counsel, power, knowledge, justice and righteousness. Who else could this have been but Yeshua?

8. The Messiah would be a prophet like Moses

⚭ Prophecy: Deuteronomy 18:15

A prophet will the LORD your God raise up to you, from the midst of you, of your brothers, like me; to him you shall hearken.

⚭ Fulfillment: John 6:14

Then those men, when they had seen the sign that Yeshua did, said, "This is truly 'the Prophet' who is to come into the world."

It is clear from the context of Deuteronomy 18:15-22 that not just one prophet was meant by Moses, but a succession of prophets that would culminate in the Messiah—"the Prophet" of Israel. By the time John the Baptist comes on the scene as the forerunner to Messiah, there was intense anticipation in Israel about the Prophet to come. The Jewish leaders asked John the Baptist if he was this prophet, to which he replied, "No" (John 1:21-25). When Philip began to follow Yeshua, he recognized Him as the One that Moses wrote about (John 1:44-45). Yeshua went on to claim that He was the One Moses wrote about (John 5:46), and many others affirmed this (John 6:14; 7:40). After Yeshua's ascension into heaven, both Peter and Stephen declared to the Jewish leaders that Yeshua was the Prophet, the Messiah, about whom Moses wrote (Acts 3:22-26; 7:37). Interestingly, no evidence to the contrary was offered by anyone in all of these accounts.

9. THE HUMILITY OF MESSIAH

◌ɔ PROPHECY: ZECHARIAH 9:9

Rejoice greatly, O daughter of Zion, shout, O daughter of Jerusalem; behold, your king comes to you, he is triumphant, and victorious, lowly, and riding upon an ass, even upon a colt the foal of an ass.

◌ɔ FULFILLMENT: JOHN 12:12-14

A great multitude when they heard that Yeshua was coming to Jerusalem, took branches of palm trees and went out to meet Him, and cried out: "Hosanna! 'Blessed is He who comes in the name of the Lord!' The King of Israel!" Then Yeshua, when

He had found a young donkey, sat on it; as it is written.

Jewish people are taught to expect a triumphant, kingly Messiah descending from heaven to rule and bring peace to the people of the earth. What is not often taught is that Messiah was first prophesied to come humbly, riding on a donkey, to accomplish His mission to reconcile us to God (Matthew 21:5-10). World peace cannot come unless individuals' hearts first find peace with God through Messiah.

According to Zechariah, the one who would enter Jerusalem was "your king," meaning Israel's king. Israel's king could be only one person, a descendant of David, which Yeshua obviously was. Yet He came first not on a warrior's steed (as He will when He returns; see Revelation 19:11-16), but humbly, as one having justice and salvation (deliverance). No one in Israel fulfilled the prophecy of Zechariah 9:9 as Yeshua did. His righteous character attracted the throngs that followed Him and listened to His teaching. His gentle humility caused children to be comfortable in His presence. This picture of Him entering Jerusalem humbly on a donkey, coupled with the following two prophetic images of Messiah— the suffering (crucified) Servant—paint a powerful picture of the totality of the life of Yeshua as Messiah.

10. THE CRUCIFIXION OF MESSIAH

✐ PROPHECY: PSALM 22

✐ FULFILLMENT: MATTHEW 27,
    MARK 15, LUKE 23, JOHN 19

Psalm 22 makes it clear that Messiah was first to come and die for the sins of the world. It is a picture of the crucifixion, years before crucifixion was a method of capital punishment. The parallels between this Psalm, written nearly 1,000 years before Jesus, and the Gospel account are uncanny.

To see the striking parallels between the prophetic imagery of a crucifixion in Psalm 22 with the facts of Yeshua's death, compare the following: His cry of anguish (Psalm 22:1; Matthew 27:46); the mocking He endured (Psalm 22:6-8; Matthew 27:39-43); the condition of His body (Psalm 22:14; compare with the condition of a person hanging on a cross); His thirst on the cross (Psalm 22:15; John 19:28); the piercing of His hands and feet on the cross (Psalm 22:16; compare with the nail prints in His hands; John 20:25-27); the gambling for His garments (Psalm 22:18; John 19:23-24). As David prefigured Messiah in so many ways, he also prefigured Him in His suffering at the hands of evildoers. Psalm 22 clearly shows that Yeshua is the crucified One of whom David wrote.

11. THE SUFFERING SERVANT

    ⌒ PROPHECY: ISAIAH 53

    ⌒ FULFILLMENT: JOHN 1:1; MATTHEW 8:16-17; 26:62-63; 27:12-14, 38, 57-60; MARK 15:27-28; LUKE 23:33; ROMANS 4:25; 1 CORINTHIANS 15:3

This is perhaps the strongest of the Messianic prophecies. The prophecy actually begins in chapter 52 verse 13. It describes the priestly ministry of the Messiah, who would die as an innocent offering for the sins of the Jewish people. The prophecy has numerous points of fulfillment recorded in the Gospel accounts of the death of the Messiah. He was "like a lamb led to the slaughter," an innocent sufferer who died on behalf of others.

As mentioned earlier, today's Jewish tradition teaches that the prophecy refers to the nation of Israel, but the text does not support this interpretation. Notice verses five and eight, where the Servant suffers for "our sins" and the "sins of my people." Someone is suffering for the sins of Israel. Therefore, the one suffering for Israel has to be someone other than Israel. It can only be Messiah. The earliest rabbinic authorities, in fact, ascribed this passage to the Messiah.

12. ISRAEL WILL MOURN

∽ PROPHECY: ZECHARIAH 12:10

And I will pour upon the house of David, and upon the inhabitants of Jerusalem, the spirit of grace and of supplication; and they shall look to Me because they have thrust him through; and they shall mourn for him, as one mourns for his only son, and shall be in bitterness for him, as one that is in bitterness for his first-born.

∽ FULFILLMENT: NOT YET FULFILLED

In the future, just before the Second Coming of Yeshua, Jewish people will recognize that He was the One "whom they pierced," and they will mourn. No human—Jew or Gentile—can be held responsible for the death of the Messiah; He died because it was the Father's plan for Him to die. In the end of days, all people will clearly see that the One whom God sent for our deliverance was Yeshua.

SOME ADDITIONAL PROPHECIES

Genesis 17:19	Psalm 118:22	Jeremiah 23:5
Numbers 24:17	Psalm 132:11	Jeremiah 31:15
Psalm 16:10	Isaiah 2:4	Hosea 11:1
Psalm 34:20	Isaiah 11:2, 10	Zechariah 3:8
Psalm 41:9	Isaiah 42:1	Zechariah 6:12
Psalm 45:2	Isaiah 50:6	Zechariah 11:12, 13
Psalm 68:18	Isaiah 59:1-6	Zechariah 13:7
Psalm 69:4, 21	Isaiah 61:1	Haggai 2:7
Psalm 110:1, 4	Isaiah 63:1	

SUGGESTED READING

Fruchtenbaum, Dr. Arnold G. *Jesus Was A Jew*. First Edition. Tustin, CA: Ariel Ministries, 2010.

Kaiser, Dr. Walter C. *Messiah in the Old Testament*. Grand Rapids, MI: Zondervan, 1995.

Pyle, Douglas. *What the Rabbonim Say about Moshiach*. New York, NY: CPM Productions, 2008.

Schlamm, Dr. J. Vera. *Pursued,* Glendale CA: Regal Books, 1972.

Telchin, Stan. *Betrayed!* Lincoln, VA: Chosen Books, 1981.

END NOTES

1 The *Haftarah* portion refers to the weekly section of Scripture read in synagogue that was selected because the Jewish sages believed there to be a congruence of the passage with the one read from the Torah. These points of connection can be thematic, lexical or grow out of a particular Jewish tradition related to the passage. Since not every passage from the Writings or the Prophets is read, it cannot be claimed with certainty that Isaiah 53 was intentionally left out.

However, it does seem unusual to end one week of readings at Isaiah 52:12 and then pick up the next week at chapter 54. When one accepts the Messianic interpretation of Isaiah 53 as fulfilled in the person of Yeshua, then the rationale for leaving out this passage is obvious. The following are the readings over the two-week period:

> *Parashah Shoftim:* Deuteronomy 16:18-21:9
> *Haftarah*: Isaiah 51:12-52:12
>
> *Parashah Ki Tetze:* Deuteronomy 21:10-25:10
> *Haftarah*: Isaiah 54:1-10

2 "Christ" is the transliteration of the Greek word "Christos," which is the same as the Hebrew "Messiah."

3 Mark Twain, "Concerning the Jews," Harper's Magazine, March 1899.

4 The repairing of the world.

5   When you beget children and grandchildren and have grown old in the land, and act corruptly and make a carved image in the form of anything, and do evil in the sight of the Lord your God to provoke Him to anger, I call heaven and earth to witness against you this day, that you will soon utterly perish from the land which you cross over the Jordan to possess; you will not prolong your days in it, but will be utterly destroyed. And the Lord will scatter you among the peoples, and you will be left few in number among the nations where the Lord will drive you. And there you will serve gods, the work of men's hands, wood and stone, which neither see nor hear nor eat nor smell. But from there you will seek the Lord your God, and you will find Him if you seek Him with all your heart and with all your soul. When you are in distress, and all these things come upon you in the latter days, when you turn to the Lord your God and obey His voice (for the Lord your God is a merciful God), He will not forsake you nor destroy you, nor forget the covenant of your fathers which He swore to them. (Deuteronomy 4:25-31)

6   If you do not carefully observe all the words of this law that are written in this book, that you may fear this glorious and awesome name, the Lord your God, then the Lord will bring upon you and your descendants extraordinary plagues—great and prolonged plagues—and serious and prolonged sicknesses. Moreover He will bring back on you all the diseases of Egypt, of which you were afraid, and they shall cling to you. Also every sickness and every plague, which is not written in this Book of the Law, will the Lord bring upon you until you are destroyed. You shall be left few in number, whereas you were as the stars of heaven in multitude, because you would not obey the voice of the Lord your God. And it shall be, that just as the Lord rejoiced over you to do you good and multiply you,

so the Lord will rejoice over you to destroy you and bring you to nothing; and you shall be plucked from off the land which you go to possess. (Deut. 28:58-63)

7   Exodus 28:13-30 describes the high-priestly ephod and the breastplate with the Urim and Thummim. It is called a "breastplate of judgment" *(hoshen ha-mishpat);* it is four-square and double; and the twelve stones were not put inside the *hoshen,* but on the outside. It is related in Leviticus 8:7-8 that when, in compliance with the command in Exodus 29:1-37, Moses consecrated Aaron and his sons as priests, "He [Moses] put upon him [Aaron] the coat, and girded him with the girdle, and clothed him with the robe, and put the ephod upon him, and he girded him with the cunningly woven band [A. V. "curious girdle"] of the ephod, and bound it unto him therewith. And he put the breastplate upon him: and in the breastplate he put the Urim and the Thummim." Deut. 33:8 (R.V.) http://www.jewishencyclopedia.com/view.jsp?artid=52&letter=U#ixzz0nafs8Jqu

8   Uzziah Son of Amaziah is called also Azariah (compare II Kings 15:1, 13, 30). He was king of Judah and began to rule at the age of 16, in the 27th year of the reign of Jeroboam II of Israel. The Book of Kings record states that his reign extended through 52 years (788-737 BCE), and that he was righteous as his father had been, though he did not take away the high places, but allowed the people to sacrifice and burn incense at them. (http://www.jewishencyclopedia.com/view.jsp?artid=65&letter=U)

9   The vision of Isaiah the son of Amoz, which he saw concerning Judah and Jerusalem in the days of Uzziah, Jotham, Ahaz, and Hezekiah, kings of Judah (Isaiah 1:1).

10 Moreover all the leaders of the priests and the people transgressed more and more, according to all the abominations of the nations, and defiled the house of the Lord which, He had consecrated in Jerusalem. And the Lord God of their fathers sent warnings to them by His messengers, rising up early and sending them, because He had compassion on His people and on His dwelling place. But they mocked the messengers of God, despised His words, and scoffed at His prophets, until the wrath of the Lord arose against His people, till there was no remedy. Therefore He brought against them the king of the Chaldeans, who killed their young men with the sword in the house of their sanctuary, and had no compassion on young man or virgin, on the aged or the weak; He gave them all into his hand. (2 Chronicles 36:14-17)

11 Isaiah 42:1-4 [9]; 49:1-6 [13]; 50:4-9[11]; 61:1-3.

12 Dr. Kaiser was educated at Brandeis University in Boston under the great Cyrus Gordon. The first evidence for the Servant being an individual is found in Isaiah 49:5-6, where the mission of the Servant is to "bring Jacob back to Him and gather Israel to Himself." Dr. Kaiser writes, "this usage of the Servant cannot be a reference to the nation of Israel, for in that case, they would be acting on themselves rather than receiving the deliverance promised to them."

Kaiser continues, "The second argument for the Servant being an individual is found in Isaiah 42:6 where the Lord has both called His servant and made Him to be a 'covenant for the people,' but if the Servant is the covenant promised to Israel, then He cannot be equated with Israel and at the same time serve Israel in this way."

A third piece of evidence is found in Isaiah 53:8, where the "servant is cut off out of the land of the living" for the sake of Israel. How then could Israel be cut off for Israel? It does not make sense to view this "servant" as the nation. It must be an individual, even a Messianic individual, because the Servant dies on behalf of the people of Israel.

A fourth reason involves the interpretation of Zechariah 3:8, written in the year 518 BCE. According to Kaiser, this verse "linked the title 'my servant' with another Messianic title, 'the Branch.'" He then argues, "If the Hebrew *tsemach*, 'Branch,' is identified with the coming 'Servant' in Isaiah 4:2; Jeremiah 23:5-6; Zechariah 6:12-13 (as it should be), then 'Servant' must also refer to the Messiah as well."

Kaiser's fifth reason for deciding against Israel being identified as the Servant is that "the description of the Servant in Isaiah 52:13-53:12 does not match the description the prophet Isaiah gave to the nation of Israel, or of any other mortals on planet earth for that matter." This is further explained in the rest of this book.

According to Kaiser, "a sixth argument would point to at least four other places in these so-called songs where they appear to distinguish between the Servant and the repentant remnant of Israel to whom the Servant ministers. Thus, in 42:3 the Servant is differentiated from the needy Israelites whom the Servant will not break or snuff out. The same phenomenon occurs in 42:6 and 49:8, where, as mentioned already, the Servant is promised that he will be made "a covenant to the people" (Israel).

13 The title "Servant of the Lord" (Hebrew: *eved Adonai),* is used of Moses seventeen times, of Joshua twice, and of David twice (in superscriptions to Ps. 18 and Ps. 36).

The last instance of this title is the one used to designate the nation of Israel and is found in Isaiah 42:19. Moses previously had referred to Abraham, Isaac and Jacob as "your [God's] servants" (Exodus 32:13; Deuteronomy 9:27; cf. also Genesis 26:24; Psalm 105:6, 42).

14 The servant/slave had a limited, involuntary tenure (six years), but could continue out of love and devotion to his master (Ex. 21:2), and the master must treat his slaves with care and respect (Ex. 21:26-27). The Servant was completely identified with his master; the work of the master was the focus and goal of the *eved's* life.

15 For more in-depth discussion, see F.F. Bruce, *The New Testament Documents: Are They Reliable?* Illinois: InterVarsity, 1983.

16 Found in Matthew 14:15-21, Mark 6:32-44, Luke 9:10-17 and John 6:1-13

17 In quotes from the NKJV, we have substituted Jesus' Hebrew name, Yeshua, for "Jesus" and his title, Messiah, for "Christ."

18 See http://www.leaderu.com/orgs/probe/docs/bib-docu.html